POETRY COMPETITION FOR 11-18 YEAR-OLDS

POP!
The Power Of Poetry

The Midlands Vol II
Edited by Donna Samworth

 Young**Writers**

First published in Great Britain in 2006 by:
Young Writers
Remus House
Coltsfoot Drive
Peterborough
PE2 9JX
Telephone: 01733 890066
Website: www.youngwriters.co.uk

SB ISBN 1 84602 387 4

Foreword

This year, the Young Writers' *POP! - The Power Of Poetry* competition proudly presents a showcase of the best poetic talent selected from thousands of up-and-coming writers nationwide.

Young Writers was established in 1991 to promote the reading and writing of poetry within schools and to the young of today. Our books nurture and inspire confidence in the ability of young writers and provide a snapshot of poems written in schools and at home by budding poets of the future.

The thought, effort, imagination and hard work put into each poem impressed us all and the task of selecting poems was a difficult but nevertheless enjoyable experience.

We hope you are as pleased as we are with the final selection and that you and your family continue to be entertained with *POP! The Midlands Vol II* for many years to come.

Contents

Bishop Vesey's Grammar School, Sutton Coldfield

Luke Finn (11) 1
Navraj Degun (11) 1
Elliott Chatham (11) 2
Raja Khan (11) 2
Benjamin Khalid (11) 3
Tadeusz Forys (11) 3
Jacob Beechey (11) 4
Matthew Gough 4
Oliver Jupp (11) 5
Callum Sandford (11) 5
Daniel Evans 6
James Ghai (11) 6
Max Hughes (12) 7
Matthew Young 7
Jack Harrington (11) 8
Mark Smyth (11) 9
Joseph Brown (11) 9
Alex Cole (12) 10

Bridgnorth Endowed School, Bridgnorth

Rebecca Sladen (12) 10
Lewis Tilley (13) 11
Amy Downes (12) 11
Beth Lautman (12) 12
Laura Proud (12) 13
Rosie Everett (12) 14
James Ellis 14
Tom Bennett (12) 15
Michael Mahony (12) 15
Francesca Edwards (12) 16
Matt McAvoy (13) 17
Costas Tsiappourdhi (12) 18
Tasha Cain (12) 19
Sophie Allan (13) 20
Gemma Wilson-Brown (12) 21
Gabrielle O'Gara (12) 22
Rose Cooper (12) 22
Laura Cowell 23

Jessica Plant (13) 23
Haydon Cardew (12) 24

Brooke School, Rugby
Class S1 24

Hasland Hall Community School, Chesterfield
Hope Thackray (12) 25

James Brindley School at Good Hope Hospital, Sutton Coldfield
Liam Jackson (11) 25
Sarah Guise (11) 26

King Edward VI College, Stourbridge
Beckie Taylor 26
Emily Butler (17) 27
Joseph Hancock (16) 28
Sam V Aldred (17) 29
Daniel William Cox (16) 30
Antonia Evans (17) 30
Andrew Perry (17) 31
Rebecca Mullen (16) 31
Michael Evans (16) 32
Matt Homer (16) 32

Meole Brace School, Shrewsbury
Kelsey Cheadle (12) 33
Seb Adams (11) 33
Katie Fletcher (15) 34
Rowan Lo (11) 35
Lizzie Stephens (15) 36
Sarah Carr (15) 37
Kim Williams (15) 38
Rachel Barton (16) 39
Tom Jones (15) 40
Abby Mills (15) 40
Sophie Palmer (15) 41
Niall Hartshorn (16) 41
Ashton Jones (15) 42
Amy Fletcher (12) 43

Naomi Wallace (14)   44
Naomi Morris (13)   45
Ryan Sargeant (13)   46
Tom Reece (13)   46
Tom Colley (12)   47
Eddy Key (15)   47
Kirsty Price (15)   48
John Andrews (11)   49
Eve Edwards (12)   50
Josh Whittaker (15)   50
Aby Edwards (15)   51
Leanne Biggs (15)   51
Georgina Evelyn Davies (11)   52
Thomas Endacott (11)   53
Benjamin Geddes (11)   54
Daniel Gilbert (11)   55
Jay Hadley (12)   56
Oliver Haines (11)   57
Leonardo Silva (11)   58
Jordan Hall (11)   59
Oliver Lane (11)   60
Lucy Lewis (11)   61
Jennifer Morgan (11)   62
Jake Rainbow (11)   63
Collette Riggs (11)   64
Samuel Rintoul (11)   65
Jodie Smith (11)   66
Lisa Clarke (12)   66
Mike André (16)   67
Tom Ashton (13)   67
Sarah Campbell (14)   68
Callum Onions (15)   69
Nadine Loach (15)   70
Jason Blakemore (15)   71
Daniela Baur (15)   72
Mark Beale (12)   73
Hanne Thorpe (16)   74
Rebecca Dowley (13)   75
Rhys Roser (12)   76
James Evans (13)   76
Joanne Hockenhull (13)   77
Stephanie Cochran (13)   78

Sophie Cooper (12)	79
Dan Pryce (12)	80
Thomas Fewtrell (12)	81
Kieran Boyes (12)	82
Nathan Hinks (12)	83
Gemma Almond (12)	84
Sally Odell (13)	85
Alice Wheeler (15)	86
Alex Tovey (12)	86
James Hickson (15)	87
Natalie Brookes (12)	87
Nahla Safwat Ashour (13)	88
Tim Farrow (12)	89
Sian Owen (12)	90
Rebecca Griffiths (12)	90
Ed Morrell (14)	91
Michael Fennell (13)	92
Becky Winwood (13)	92
Elsie Cinnamond (12)	93
Ross O'Callaghan (12)	93
Ailsa Young (12)	94
Gemma Cusack (14)	95
Jessica Morgan (12)	96
William Royle (13)	96
Tracy Stott (12)	97
Gary Smith (12)	97
Owen Kelly (14)	98
Lyle Sambrook (12)	99
Siân Lloyd (13)	100
Charlie Louise Davidson (11)	101
Ed Speller (13)	102
Damon Jones	103
Rosie Corsentino (12)	104
Jack Sanders (13)	104
Sara O'Callaghan (12)	105
Aron Davies (13)	105
Sophie Bishop (13)	106
Megan Wood (13)	106
Andy Dunn (13)	107
Lauren Owen (13)	107
Kyle Arrowsmith (14)	108
David Howarth (13)	109

Anna Davies (14)   110
Will Alexander (13)   110
Andrew Kirby (15)   111
Paige Walford (13)   111
Tineka Frost (12)   112
Poppy Olah (14)   112
Lucie James (14)   113
Tom Bowen (13)   114
Abbygale Lewis (13)   115
Robin Kearney (15)   116
Alex Edwards (12)   117
Ben Williams (12)   118
David Alexander (13)   118
Charlotte Jones (12)   119
Lowell John (12)   119
Toby Pierce (12)   120
Anna Pemblington (12)   121
Sophie Putterill (12)   122

Rutland College, Oakham
Rachael Hollingsworth (16)   122
Meryl Harland (17)   123
Sean Doyle (16)   123
Thomas Jackson, Joe Harley (16) & George Shelbourn (17) 124
Kelly Pridmore (16)   125
Charlotte Reidy (17)   126
Alex Addison (17)   126
Emily Wilce (16)   127
Kayleigh Dolby (16)   127
Charlotte Mills (16)   128
Rozie Burgoyne McPhee (18)   129
Daniel Wateridge (16)   130
Harriet Bell (16)   131
Sian Webb (16)   132
Fuchsia Wilkins (17)   133
Hannah Morrison (16)   134
James Statham (17)   135

Small Heath School & Sixth Form, Birmingham
Jaweria Iqbal (12)   136
Hafsah Ali (12)   136

Rehana Hussain (12)   137
Jasmin Begum (13)   137
Ayesha Kausar Hussain (12)   138
Umeh Humaira Yousaf (12)   138
Mohammed Nasir (13)   139
Aishah Ahmed (12)   139
Akeem Forrest (13)   140
Yousuf Ali (12)   140
Iram Naaz Qureshi (12)   141
Adnan Khalid (12)   141
Misbah Ahmed (13)   142
Aseel Mahmood (12)   142
Aisha Mohammed (12)   143
Hassan Hussain (13)   143
Wahida Begum (12)   144
Zain-Al-Abedeen Banares (12)   144
Shaista Hussain (12)   145
Shamima Akhtar (12)   145
Ruqayyah Noor (12)   146
Nasir Ali (13)   146

Southam College, Southam
Andrew Barnes (11)   147
Leo Parkinson (11)   148

Studley High School, Studley
Andrew King (13)   148
Anna Padfield (13)   149
Maddy Howells (11)   149
Jennifer Priestley (13)   150
Benjamin Costello (14)   151
Ellie Springer (12)   152
Naomi Layton (13)   153
Tasmin Jones (13)   154
Mustafa Razzak (11)   154
Richard Hyett (13)   155
Kate Dodds (11)   155
Becky Innes (13)   156
Gemma Simmons (13)   157
Mandy Spires (13)   157
Ruth Foster (13)   158

The National School CE Technology College, Hucknall

Rebecca Hoy (14)	158
Katherine Asbury (12)	159
Reece Sanders (13)	159
Shan Thompson (13)	160
Lawrence Anthony Turton (13)	160
Sarah Falconer (15)	161
Kayleigh Abbott (15)	161
Chris Hibbard (12)	162
Jordan White (12)	162
Jasmin Bear (11)	163
Thomas Sellars (11)	163
Sarah Dunstan (12)	164
Chelsea Davis (12)	165
Anna Johnson (13)	166
Ashley Vere (12)	166
Gemma Wayte (11)	167
Sally Danby (13)	167
Arlene Ndiweni (12)	168
Kayleigh Henson (12)	168
Christopher Hunt (12)	169
Jaide Croll (12)	170
Lauren Sketchley (12)	170
Dominic Johnson (13)	171
Holly Jemmett-Allen (11)	172
George Bentley (11)	172
John Maiden (11)	173
Andrew Jowitt (11)	173
Luke Tait (13)	174
Harry Petcher (12)	175
Nicola Burton (11)	176
Charlotte Wadsworth (12)	176
Ffion Naylor-Roberts (12)	177
Tim Maiden (16)	178
Nicola Jenner (14)	179
Jessica Bestwick (11)	180
Ashton Mayes (13)	180
Nicola Maiden (14)	181
Sophie Platts (12)	181
Danielle Abbott (11)	182

The Summerhill School, Kingswinford

Amie Bottley (11)	182
Selena Malone (11)	183
Rylie Jones (11)	183
Luke Breakwell (11)	184
Scott Adam Wassell (12)	185
Ellie Oldacre (11)	186
Harry Beasley (12)	186
Chloé Travers (11)	187
Andrew Randle (11)	188
Sophie Ball (11)	189
Anna Stewart (11)	190
Theo Barfoot (11)	191
Jade Wilde (11)	192
Beth Rogerson (11)	193
Robin Rossmann (11)	194
Charlotte Turner (11)	195
Nick Page (11)	196
James Hill (11)	197

The Wakeman School, Shrewsbury

Paige Korbel (13)	198
James Pereira (12)	199
John France (14)	200

Thomas Telford School, Telford

Ryan Flannery (12)	200
Mitchell Hill (12)	201
Chloe Simister (12)	201
Kate Marshall (13)	202
Kirsty Harris (11)	202
Jack Leech (12)	203
Laura Roper (12)	203
Nathan Sanghera (12)	204
Warren Beards (12)	204
Hayley Davies (12)	205
Rebecca Percox (12)	205
Lara Vail (12)	206
Katie Moreton (11)	206
Holly Wild (12)	207
Olivia Walmsley (12)	207

Melissa Nock (11)   208
Georgia Christodoulou (12)   209
Stephanie Rogers (12)   210
Amy Finch (12)   210
Luke Hughes (12)   211
Curtis Goodman (12)   211
Samantha Beresford (12)   212
Emma Tranter (12)   212
Alistair Smith (11)   213
Jake Megal (11)   213
Kyle Baker (12)   214
Hurneet Kaur Kalirai (11)   215
Jade Brownhill (11)   216
Andrea Field (12)   217
Kellie Appleby (13)   217
Lily Penfold (12)   218
Abbie Bailey (11)   218
Danielle Bowater (11)   219
Kalpna Ahir (13)   219
Vicki Wood (12)   220
Tyler Thomas (11)   220
Liam Sullivan (12)   221
Rachael Holyhead (12)   222
Daniel Goodall (13)   223
Samantha Lunn (11)   223
Shazia Bano-Shah (12)   224
Kate Breeze (12)   224
Reece Smith (12)   225
Emmie Edwards (11)   225
Gemma Maybury (11)   226
Stuart Dunlop (11)   227
Laura Roberts (11)   228
Carly-Jade Newnes (12)   228

Trinity Catholic School, Leamington Spa
Alex Davies (13)   229
Katie O'Kelly (13)   229
Hannah Quayle (13)   230
Nandylola Lloyd (13)   230
Jessica Clack (13)   231
Lilly Aaron (12)   231

Dulcie McFadden (13)   232
David Myers Nava (13)   232
Sarah-Jane Wilson (13)   233
Zoe Ransley (13)   233
Lee Sharpe (13)   233
Sinead Healy (13)   234
Jacob Reed (13)   234
Aimee Scanlon (14)   235
Kayleigh Randall (12)   235
Emily Murphy (13)   236
Arthur Bradley (13)   236
Katherine Horrocks (13)   236
Alex Norman (12)   237
Kayleigh Walsh (13)   237
Harley Stanley (13)   237
Lewis Bromwich (12)   238
Lianne Davis (12)   238
Daniel Brennan (12)   239
Ryan Billington (12)   239
Lucio-Tommaso Abinanti (13)   240
George Coady (13)   240
James Lawless (12)   241
Keir Sayce (13)   241
Archie Skelcher (13)   241
Mitchell Morris (12)   242
Shannon Marie Byrne (12)   242
Lauren Ransford (12)   243

Woodfield Middle School, Redditch
Nicole Corrigan (12)   244
Mariya Arshad (12)   244
Daniella Gregg (11)   245
Jayna Chauhan (12)   245
Bradley Jones (11)   245
Leigh Todd & Jodie Bough (12)   246
Cassie Larkin (12) & James King (13)   247
Ben Hyde (11)   248
Dale Seel (11)   248
Danielle Fenton (12)   249

Woodlands Community School, Derby

Grace Farrington (15)	249
Katy Harlow (14)	250
Kate Turner (16)	251
Julian Esposito (15)	252
Emily Boyer (15)	253

The Poems

Brandon Point

We stood at the bottom of Brandon Point,
A mighty wind was blowing,
The sea frothed and bubbled so much,
You'd think that it was snowing!

So up we went, along the path,
Towards a lonely shelter,
From there we watched the seagulls soar
And tumble helter-skelter!

Advancing through the boggy marsh,
We ventured past the stiles,
We reached the top, we stood in awe,
For we could see for miles!

So back we went, a breathless rush,
Slowly nearing the finish,
We finally got back in the car
And into the bar for a Guinness!

Luke Finn (11)
Bishop Vesey's Grammar School, Sutton Coldfield

My Dream Car!

I have got a Ferrari and I hate Barbie.
Its colour is red and it always goes to bed.
It always beams and that's why I see it in my dreams.
That is my dream car!

I have got a Lamborghini and it's my genie.
Its colour is black and it doesn't lack.
It always plays 'tig' and its owner wears a wig.
That is my dream car!

I have got a Porsche and it goes faster than my horse.
Its colour is blue and it is two.
It's got a brain of its own and it always breaks its bone.
That is my dream car!

That is my dream car!

Navraj Degun (11)
Bishop Vesey's Grammar School, Sutton Coldfield

Space

Up, up in the blackness,
What could there be?

A spaceman in a shiny suit,
In Apollo 3.

Planets, planets,
Where do they go?

They circle around
In their own magic show.

Why do comets whizz
Through the air?

To leave their stardust
Everywhere.

Back down to Earth
What will I say?

I would like to go there
Another day.

Elliott Chatham (11)
Bishop Vesey's Grammar School, Sutton Coldfield

Food Is Great

Food is great,
It decides your weight
Many fruits are put in crates.
Chocolate bars and creamy cakes
Chicken burgers and chicken steak
Sugary sweets and other various treats
Different types of breads that you can eat
Chips are great
But if you eat too much you'll put on weight
So take my words
Food is great!

Raja Khan (11)
Bishop Vesey's Grammar School, Sutton Coldfield

My Art Poem

Art is a subject at all the schools,
But not a subject for extreme fools.
Here is one such occasion
And they got expelled just for that,
So listen carefully for it's a fact.

It started off a normal day,
With peace and harmony in every way.
For it was art today, what a treat,
We were inside away from the heat.
But when we entered we had a fright,
The classroom looked like a bomb site.

The names of the culprits were painted on the wall,
Space among the debris was very small.
Eggs had been smashed on the chairs
And there was a huge mess everywhere.

To this day they are cleaning up the mess,
But what the job pays is anyone's guess.

Benjamin Khalid (11)
Bishop Vesey's Grammar School, Sutton Coldfield

Untitled

It's Christmas Eve already
and I'm watching that Christmas tree!
Looking for Santa's presents
but there are none for me.
I know, I'll send him an email.
I've waited for hours on end but
there is no reply.
Do you think he's trying to ignore me?
I was very good you see
it really was not my fault
I drove Dad's car into that tree.

Tadeusz Forys (11)
Bishop Vesey's Grammar School, Sutton Coldfield

The Worst School In The World

The worst school in the world,
On my first day I hurled,
I've been there for nearly a year,
The teachers shout so loud I can barely hear.

School finishes at 8.59,
Then we start again a minute later at nine,
If you dare be late,
You'll end up like Billy; the boy Miss Rex ate.

The toilet is in the ground,
It probably costs less than a pound,
The headmistress has a moustache
And the secretary ran off with all her cash.

The lessons are taught in the dungeons
And the teachers look like the ugly Star Wars Gunguns,
The school is guarded by electric fences,
But we don't know the reasons for these defences.

If you think that my school is cool,
Then you must have brains made of drool,
All the reasons above just show why my school is not cool
And that's why they call it the world's worst school.

Jacob Beechey (11)
Bishop Vesey's Grammar School, Sutton Coldfield

My Slave Grandad

Here are the words as the old wise man told.
He told me Timmy Walker not to get cold.
He also told me soon he would be sold.
Alone I am with my blanket wrapped around,
Waiting to hear his voice, that wonderful sound.

Without my grandpa my heart beats so slow,
My body has lots its rhythm,
My body has lost its flow.

Matthew Gough
Bishop Vesey's Grammar School, Sutton Coldfield

Fast And Furious

Roaring of engines,
Stationary and waiting for one word.

Slam down the accelerator,
Speed rising, rising.
Screeching of tyres,
Smoke bellowing.

Gripping tightly,
Hands aching,
Vibration tingling,
Head buzzing,
Concentration level maximum.

Moving up the field,
Closer, closer,
Swerve left,
Overtake,
Swerve right,
Overtake.

Three more corners,
Chequered flag,
In the distance,
Heart pounding,
One aim,
One goal,
Win!

Oliver Jupp (11)
Bishop Vesey's Grammar School, Sutton Coldfield

Death

D arkness rules this land
E rasing you with its invisible hand
A ny time it will take your mind
T easing you with its horrid chime
H urtling through endless space.

Callum Sandford (11)
Bishop Vesey's Grammar School, Sutton Coldfield

Jasper Jasper

Jasper, Jasper, you're my cat,
You eat too much that's why you're fat,
Pouncing on a shed, jumping for joy,
Playing with your mousey toy.

What do you think when you get fed
In your beautiful little head?
He replies, 'I love you Dan
Because I'm your biggest fan.'

Lying by the fire all day long,
Why's your tail big and long?
'Jasper let's play mouse, oh no you've won,
Let's play again, that was fun!'

Jasper, you're so polite!
Have you ever had a fight?
Why do you get on my bed
And cuddle up by my ted?

Why do you always purr
With your stacks of ginger fur?
I love you, you love me,
We are all a big family.

Daniel Evans
Bishop Vesey's Grammar School, Sutton Coldfield

My Poem

Bishop Vesey's is my school
And I think it's really cool!
This school is one of the best
Much better than all the rest!
We have many different subjects in Bishop Vesey's
Some are hard and some are easy!
There are some strict teachers and some fun,
Which lessons are boring? . . . None!
This is better than my other schools!
Because Bishop Vesey's *rules!*

James Ghai (11)
Bishop Vesey's Grammar School, Sutton Coldfield

The Great Trolley Race

The great trolley race is about to begin,
With the wheels greased and the drivers ready,
Lined up on the starting line,
Preparing for the race of the century
And then the klaxon bellows
And they're off,
As they skid, yoghurts spill,
As the drivers have their fill
Yet as the race draws to its final stages,
The shop's tattered and trashed,
It came,
The greatest hurdle of them all,
The stop,
All of them break
But not quick enough . . .
And all that's said is,
'Mess in aisle 4!'

Max Hughes (12)
Bishop Vesey's Grammar School, Sutton Coldfield

My iPod

My iPod is really brill,
When I'm stressed it helps me chill.
Whether I'm on the move or in my bed,
I've always got music in my head!

AAC is the one for me,
Although, MP3 makes me smile with glee.
I get my tracks off Apple Online,
Which can be from the ordinary to the sublime.

I love my iPod, I use it every day,
It does make the battery go down,
But that's OK!

Matthew Young
Bishop Vesey's Grammar School, Sutton Coldfield

Brothers, Who'd Have 'Em?

I am the middle son
In my family
Doesn't that sound fun?
But I have to disagree.

My older brother laughs and jokes,
When he's not fighting me.
My younger one kicks and pokes,
When he thinks Mum can't see.

I've had bruises and a black eye,
Broken toys and games.
They play the PS games I buy
And never get the blame.

Dad and Mum try to be fair.
I know they try quite hard.
When one or the other pulls my hair,
They show the red card.

There are good things I must say,
Like wrestling, chess and rugby
And someone to chat to about my day
And beating them at Monopoly.

We drive our parents mad
When rolling on the floor.
All in all I'm not too sad
Although the dog hides by the door.

Sometimes I would love to be the only one,
But I know I would miss out.
I'd end up a lonely one
And miss my brothers without doubt.

Jack Harrington (11)
Bishop Vesey's Grammar School, Sutton Coldfield

My Poem

My poem will be the best,
Much better than all the rest,
I'll fly high into the air,
People criticise it if they dare!
Oh yes, oh yes, oh yes
My poem will be the best.

The judges will think it's great,
Better than Jamie Tate's.
It'll be fancy, it'll be fun,
Oh yes and the odd pun!
With lots of rhyme
And of course all in time.

My poem will be the best,
Better than all the rest.
Oh yes, oh yes, oh yes!

Mark Smyth (11)
Bishop Vesey's Grammar School, Sutton Coldfield

I Can't Write Poems!

I can't write poems,
I think they're really hard,
When I sit in English I don't know where to start.

I can't write poems.

When I sit and think,
My brain just seems to shrink.

I can't write poems.

Others in the class,
They think it's a piece of cake,
When they put pen to paper,
They never make a mistake.

I can't write poems.

Joseph Brown (11)
Bishop Vesey's Grammar School, Sutton Coldfield

My Dearest Grandad

My dearest grandad is lovely
He is very old and frail
He has grey hair and his skin is pale

His favourite hobby is driving his rusty car
Which is old, silver and slow
But he doesn't care because he just goes with the flow

He used to be a policeman in his youth
And regularly shows me his medals
Which are made of different shiny metals

He adores my brother, Danny and me
And always talks of the old times
When he chased robbers and gave them heavy fines

He loves his garden so much
And spends most of his spare time working in it
He doesn't like us playing on it cos he has a fit.

Alex Cole (12)
Bishop Vesey's Grammar School, Sutton Coldfield

The Train

Horns hooting as we go
When we start we go slow
Speeding quickly through the town
Over hills up and down
Not a human in sight
It is turning dark and will soon be night.

The sun alight once more
In the sky the birds soar
Through the city we pass
We see no fields, hills or grass
The journey comes to a sudden end
There are no corners, no more bends.

Rebecca Sladen (12)
Bridgnorth Endowed School, Bridgnorth

I Wonder

I wonder why the sky is so blue.
I wonder why it rains.
I wonder if Heaven is true.
I wonder why we have windowpanes.

I wonder why we have wars.
I wonder what happens when you die.
I wonder why some people slam doors.
I wonder what makes you cry.

I wonder how nature works.
I wonder how many stars there are.
I wonder why there are so many jerks.
I wonder what's the point of a golfing par.

I wonder why I'm writing this.
I wonder who is reading this.
I wonder why I'm wondering this.
I wonder who you are.

Lewis Tilley (13)
Bridgnorth Endowed School, Bridgnorth

Untitled

Sitting upon the greenhouse,
Whilst patiently waiting, the cat saw a mouse
The mouse was quite fat and rather slow
When all of a sudden, *oh no!*
The cat saw the mouse
And the mouse saw the cat.
Then just like that
The cat got up at quite a pace.
The mouse had seen and the cat gave chase
Around the garden they ran for a while
When out of nowhere came a tile
The cat soon ended up in bed.
When the mouse pushed a roof tile onto his head.

Amy Downes (12)
Bridgnorth Endowed School, Bridgnorth

Emotions

Loneliness
The lonely girl drags her feet,
Along the deserted street.
Searching through the bins each dark night,
For something, anything to bite.
Loneliness.

Happiness
The happy girl skips cheerfully through the busy park,
With her mum behind and her dog Mark.
Pizza, chips, lemonade and chocolate ice cream for tasty lunch,
She always has something scrumptious to munch.
Happiness.

Sadness
The sad, upset girl lies helplessly on her bed,
Crying because of what someone mean said.
She does not want to face any kind of food,
Because she has been put in a bad mood.
Sadness.

Excitement
The excited girl loudly screams as the roller coaster plunges,
Is she going to land in the slimy gunges?
It's birthday time, extra yummy sweets and cake,
Presents, jewellery and things to make.
Excitement.

Beth Lautman (12)
Bridgnorth Endowed School, Bridgnorth

The Eggshell

The wind took off with the sunset
The fog came up with the tide
When the demon found an eggshell
Only to find that inside -
A faint figure seemed to stand
The demon scooped it up by hand
'Who are you?' the demon queried
And the small figure replied wearied
'Because of the opening of the eggshell, the spirits have all
                                                    been let free
And now you must suffer the consequences by coming and
                                                    joining me.

The wind fell dead with the midnight
The fog disappeared in a flash
When the demon was inside the eggshell
Waiting for the day of its dash
Not the slightest sound was heard
And the demon didn't speak a word
But he knew he was prisoner and
Wouldn't see daylight and
Because of the opening of the eggshell, the spirits had all been let free
And the demon suffered the consequences by coming and joining
                                                    the . . .

Laura Proud (12)
Bridgnorth Endowed School, Bridgnorth

The Human

It's raining
Tears are falling down so heavily
The human floods.

It's a storm
Be careful of the human
Her anger has been released.

Why is the human blaming things on life?
Life is only natural, it can't be controlled.

It's misty,
The world is not appearing today.
She has a spot on her nose.

It's hot,
The human has finally grabbed happiness,
Love is all around.

But when the love has died,
So does the human.
The human is no more.

Rosie Everett (12)
Bridgnorth Endowed School, Bridgnorth

The Calling

In the dark and in the blue,
Someone there is watching you,
In amongst the cries and growls,
Lies the wickedness of the howls,
Twigs a-crunching, trees a-shaking,
Animals munching, people quaking,
In beneath the mist and fog,
Lies the curse of the wicked dog,
Birds up high, ghosts down low,
See the curse of the pumpkin glow.
Snakes a-slithering, spiders a-crawling,
See the curse of the dead man calling . . .

James Ellis
Bridgnorth Endowed School, Bridgnorth

Schooldays

Our bus journey's bad
from the clear country air
to the drone of the town
going to school does make me frown

Sums and equations
left and right
Mr Middleton's
always right

We go all the way
for five lessons a day
when finally we leave
a sigh of relief we heave

Forever on time
never be late
wait for the bell
to escape from the hell.

Tom Bennett (12)
Bridgnorth Endowed School, Bridgnorth

Moving On

I don't want to let it go, I won't.
It's my identity, it's who I am.
This whole life, which I ran.
It's my world, it's all I know.
It's all here, but I must go.

I don't see how I can leave,
But all I can do now is grieve.
Though it's not the end, I'm only ten.
My old life's gone but it starts again.

Acceptance creeps through me at last.
I must move on, it's in the past.
My family's here, the ones I trust.
I don't want to move on, but I must.

Michael Mahony (12)
Bridgnorth Endowed School, Bridgnorth

The Oversized Kid

One dark, gloomy night
There was a monster
Who gave everybody such a fright,
He was tall
He was hairy
And his favourite food was,
Gruel?

This monster, I say, was barely scary
But once his tummy grumbled
He wasn't exactly a fairy,
He would growl
He would roar
And the worst thing he did was,
Howl?

So as you can see
He's not so bad
He's just like an oversized kid
Who never grew up,
Into a lad.

Francesca Edwards (12)
Bridgnorth Endowed School, Bridgnorth

My Poem About Spaghetti

Spaghetti is so tasty
It is such a pleasure to eat
Covered in rich sauce
And very tender meat

Sprinkled with mountains of cheese
To add an extra touch
Spaghetti is so tasty
You can never have too much

There's so many ways to eat it
You can shovel it down your gob
But when people see you
They think you're such a slob

Though there's another way to eat it
This method is rather slow
But if you've got the time
Suck it down your throat

You can twirl it round your fork
This may be hard for some
But once you get the hang of it
It becomes really fun.

Matt McAvoy (13)
Bridgnorth Endowed School, Bridgnorth

Technology Is Changing

Television, computers
And DVDs.
Instead of tapes
We've got Mp3s.
Technology is changing.

Mobile phones
They're not just for ringing.
Send texts and take pictures
They're all-dancing, all-singing.
Technology is changing.

Now you don't need books
To find the facts you need.
Just search the net,
It takes too long to read.
Technology is changing.

As technology evolves
New jargon must be made,
Like texting, gigabytes and ram
These words are here to stay.
Technology is changing.

Technology is changing
There's no denying it.
I can't wait to see
How it will change bit by bit.

Costas Tsiappourdhi (12)
Bridgnorth Endowed School, Bridgnorth

Cat's Tale!

I'm not a house cat
I am a wild cat
I love to explore the great outdoors
Not sitting at home washing my paws

Out through the cat flap
Not for a cat nap
Out chasing leaves
No fuss please

I'd rather climb trees
Than chase buzzing bees
It's fun to run and jump about,
Then stop a while and fish for trout

It's getting dark
Have I got time to chase the lark?
My tummy is rumbling
No time for tumbling

But I'm a wild cat
And proud of that
I'll have to catch my own tea
But oh, I'm so hungry

That's it, I'm going in
I'm going to get my din-din
I'm not a wild cat
I am a house cat.

Tasha Cain (12)
Bridgnorth Endowed School, Bridgnorth

My Pets

I have a cat called Tilly,
My mum says she's really silly,
She sits in the road,
Outside our abode,
It's no wonder she gets so chilly.

Then she comes through the door,
Drops a mouse on the floor,
She takes it to bed,
But it's not always dead,
So it ends up all blood and gore.

I have a pony called Cass,
She eats far too much grass,
Which makes her so fat,
Just like my grey cat,
But she's still my favourite lass.

I give her carrots to eat,
When she's earned a nice treat,
Walked down the lane,
Or I've combed her mane
And she hasn't stood on my feet.

Sophie Allan (13)
Bridgnorth Endowed School, Bridgnorth

Deep Inside Our Minds

Despair is there to haunt you,
To weigh you down like stone.
His mouth speaks, hisses and taunts,
In a frightful, chilling tone.

Courage is loyal and fearless,
With spirits and hopes so high.
He speaks words of encouragement,
Whenever you pass by.

Stress is nothing but evil,
A deeply devilish foe.
He'll make you hot and bothered,
Angry from head to toe.

Strength is there to help you,
Out of all those sticky situations.
He'll help you get past obstacles,
To reach your destination.

Fear is there to scare you,
To make you cry and moan,
She'll make you feel outnumbered,
Upset, weak and alone.

Success is there to greet you,
When you finally reach the end.
You'll have tackled every obstacle,
Struggled round every bend.

These friends and foes are feelings,
But these are just a few.
They live deep inside our minds,
Deep inside me and you.

Gemma Wilson-Brown (12)
Bridgnorth Endowed School, Bridgnorth

Dropping It

I went there,
My head filled with questions,
Will I do it?
Is it possible?
My blood rushing,
Too fast to bear,
I was filled from the hairs on my head to the tips of my toes,
Anxiousness,
Waiting, waiting,
When can I go?
I heard voices behind me,
'She'll never do it.'
'How can she?'
Hairs on end,
My heart thumping,
Like someone continually punching me in the chest,
Leaving the comments behind me,
I went,
Dropping it,
But dropping what?

Gabrielle O'Gara (12)
Bridgnorth Endowed School, Bridgnorth

The Prisoner

Heart thumping like the steady beat of a drum,
Footsteps getting closer.
Not looking back for fear of what I will see,
Got to keep going, got to get free.
My own footsteps ringing in my ears,
Turning down alleyways and paths alike.
Confused, not knowing where to run,
Lost,
I stumble,
A shot . . . silence.

Rose Cooper (12)
Bridgnorth Endowed School, Bridgnorth

The Sea

I am happy today, lovely and calm,
Only crashing near the beach.
I hold the boats upon my skin,
While giving the surfers a bumpy ride.

Today I am angry, raving and crashing,
I claim the lives of a few.
Crashing on the rocks,
As I sweep people far from home.

As the day gets older,
I eat the beach away.
Washing away the sandcastles,
Washing away the day that has just gone.

Every day I am here,
Why not come and call in?
If they ask who you're looking for,
Then just answer, 'The sea.'

Laura Cowell
Bridgnorth Endowed School, Bridgnorth

Sea Snail

S nail
L umbering around the ocean bed
O bstacles gather in my way
W andering, lonely

S nail
E asy-going life
A s I search for a friend

S nail
N eedn't go so fast
A s a speeding sea horse
I hide in the coral reef
L abyrinth of ocean colour.

Jessica Plant (13)
Bridgnorth Endowed School, Bridgnorth

My Life Is In The Middle Of An Endless Night

I am part of you,
But how can that be true?
My life is in the middle of an endless night.
I never bother to try,
Because most of the time you lie,
My life is in the middle of an endless night.
I don't know what to do,
Should I bother to see you?
My life is in the middle of an endless night.
We are not the same,
But none of us is to blame,
My life, my life, an endless night . . .

Haydon Cardew (12)
Bridgnorth Endowed School, Bridgnorth

Bonfire Night

B rilliant Bonfire Night, it's exciting
O *ohs* and *aahhs*
N oisy people, fire and fireworks
F rightened children and little dogs
I can see fireworks in the sky, they go *bang*
R *attle, boom, bang, pop, crackle and whizz*
E veryone is cheering

N ear the bonfire it's very hot
I hold a sparkler
G oing round the twisters whistle
H ot dogs, sausages, jacket potatoes and toffee apples
T ime to go home.

Class S1
Brooke School, Rugby

Hurricane Katrina

Children screaming, writhing in pain,
Walls collapsing, foundations broke,
Floods washing over them, torrents of rain,
Towering infernos, going up in smoke.

Walls collapsing, foundations broke,
People are fleeing, pillars toppling in,
Towering infernos, going up in smoke,
Like the Devil's come back, committing more sin.

People are fleeing, pillars toppling in,
Animals drowning, belongings washed away,
Like the Devil's come back, committing more sin,
Disasters like this, we wish someone would pay.

Animals drowning, belongings washed away,
Floods washing over them, torrents of rain,
Disasters like this, we wish someone would pay,
Children screaming, writhing in pain.

Hope Thackray (12)
Hasland Hall Community School, Chesterfield

The Drip

T he doctor explained why I had to go to hospital.
'H elp Mum, I might need a drip.'
E mergency room here I come.

D ad drives me to hospital.
R oom full of doctors here to help me, but still I'm scared.
I f only they could take the pain away, but still
   they don't know what's going on.
P ain relief at last, some rest and then I am good to go.

Liam Jackson (11)
James Brindley School at Good Hope Hospital, Sutton Coldfield

The Needle

'I need the magic cream,' I demanded!
'You'll be fine,' Mum retorted.
'No Mum. I need the
magic cream, now!'
'Stop being so silly and
let the nurse do what
she's got to do.'
The nurse came with
her cotton wool and a
bright red plaster.
I cried out with a yelp
and then that was over
and done with. Was
it really worth all the fuss?
As I
dropped
off to
sleep.
z
z
z.

Sarah Guise (11)
James Brindley School at Good Hope Hospital, Sutton Coldfield

Future

How can we speak of the future?
For the future does not exist.
It's simply a collection of hopes and dreams,
Of which we've no power to resist.

Beckie Taylor
King Edward VI College, Stourbridge

Future

'To lose you is to never love again . . .'

She stares into the glass
Wondering what she'll see today
The broken heart of what's come to pass
Or the pain of the things that may

It's not the same since he left
She feels she's been ripped in two
And one half, the better half, left with him
With the other not knowing who

She is, or what she'll be
If he really has just gone
Stay and pine, live half her life
Or cut her loss, just move on

She cut her loss that's true enough
The scars still haunt her skin
But as the crimson flows, she knows
It will always be this, without him

Where will she be in ten years' time?
The pain never really goes
It's not a life, it's half a life
But at least with time, it barely shows

She'll move, from boy to boy
Never really loving a single one
They'll never be him, they'll never love her
Never replace the one she lost, he's gone

The pain is fading fast now
The lights grow slowly dim
And as she dies she thinks of her love, of how
My future really died with him.

Emily Butler (17)
King Edward VI College, Stourbridge

The Future

Good morning, it's the future
And you can't get out of bed.
I'm afraid for that, you'll need insurance,
So be careful where you tread.

The petrol has long since run out
But people sit in queues.
To fill their tanks with happy thoughts
Then don their walking shoes.

Not being politically correct
Is now against the law.
So nobody says anything,
They just hope for good rapport.

The teens, now anorexic,
Called 'obese' for all those years.
Fat camp is, now 'Chubb Up',
But the media still sneers.

People fall in the street
And try to sue the ground.
The ground did not turn up for court
A verdict was never found.

The East is now America,
And is split up into states.
When we die, we go to Disneyland
And not the pearly gates.

The future is a quiet place
The past, it will be, soon.
Earthly problems, will be of little thought,
For we'll all live on the moon.

Joseph Hancock (16)
King Edward VI College, Stourbridge

Jerusalem Lost

Tomorrow draws us ever closer
To that seemingly inevitable time,
When the death of hope
Sees the birth of reason
And the rise of Nietzsche's dream.

When Man shall at last be freed
Of the shackles of conformity
And the chains of blind faith,
With a new age of fact over fiction,
Of blinding light over darkness.

And we shall emerge liberated.
Gone the bad old days
Of holy wars and begging forgiveness
For sins that seem, well, outdated
And we shall be . . . happy.

Time drags us ever nearer,
Relentlessly to that neon dawn,
That pseudo-emancipation
When they declare Darwin was right
And the five thousand were tricked.

And life shall go on
Much the same as before
With childhood turning full circle:

But with nothing to live for,
And nothing to strive for,
And nothing left to die for.

Sam V Aldred (17)
King Edward VI College, Stourbridge

Remember The Future

Do you remember the future?
When, driven by aspirations of grandeur,
We would gaze up at the stars
And believe we were amongst them.
When we craved money,
We just took it.
When we dreamed of success,
Greed drove us to it.
When we desired power,
They conformed to our regime.
There are only us, and them.
The only difference is
Where that metaphorical dart strikes.
It hit their hearts, as it hit our back pockets
And crushed all compassion within.
For our names shall cease to prosper,
And we will pay for our sin.

Daniel William Cox (16)
King Edward VI College, Stourbridge

Recycled

(Inspired by 'Sonnet 18' by Shakespeare)

Dare I compare thee to a summer's day?
Thou art more scorching and so venomous,
Tempests do sweep the cities away
And with gathering hast thou art more merciless;
Sometime from our own coasts we are chased,
And often into icy currents we are spun,
All because we would not forfeit, we raced
We reached on foolishly. Now we are done.
But thy relentless ferocity shall not fade,
Till our crops are limp, our trees are choked,
Till the debts of our stupidity we have paid,
And our air, with poison, is enveloped.
So whilst we know that thou art grave,
Why can we not think of what we could save?

Antonia Evans (17)
King Edward VI College, Stourbridge

Ripples

The future, stretching out before us like a spiralling web.
Each strand branches, each action we take has a consequence.
With one tiny movement the future is changed,
One drop in the pool creating hundreds of ripples.

The future, always in the distance; never quite 'right now'.
Travelling towards us then disappearing without a trace.
Now living what, yesterday, seemed like tomorrow,
Watching the future weave its way into the past.

The future, seconds ticking and chopping the future short.
Next month will soon be tomorrow, a decade falls into next week.
Drifting along the paths ahead of us,
Choosing our steps and watching us mold our own destinies.

The future, what the hell eh? Don't think about it.
It's unavoidable; tomorrow will still be there when you wake up.
Just live for the present, wedged safely between future and past.
Walking along the strands, creating a billion ripples.

Andrew Perry (17)
King Edward VI College, Stourbridge

Poem About The Future

The sun sets in the dark night sky,
Storm clouds silently drift by,
Rain pours down on the dusty ground,
No creature left to make a sound,
Flash of lightning glows in the night,
The fat round moon reflecting the light,
Glaciers melting, the sea starts to flood,
Soaking the land, turning to mud,
Global warming, it's up to you,
The future depends on what you do.

Rebecca Mullen (16)
King Edward VI College, Stourbridge

The Future - A Series Of Haikus

The future, unformed,
Like sea water, mutable,
Unpredictable.

Yet patterns emerge,
Expressed in waves, wind, science,
Quantifiable.

But not quite certain,
With human will, all things bend
To suit selection.

Choice can shape our world,
Order keeps the status quo,
Equilibrium.

Such is real life,
Pattern versus decision,
Forging the future.

Michael Evans (16)
King Edward VI College, Stourbridge

The Future

In the future   poverty
In the future   hope
In the future   death
In the future   new life
In the future   hatred
In the future   passion
In the future   disease
In the future   cures
In the future   disaster
In the future   elation

The future in our hands.

Matt Homer (16)
King Edward VI College, Stourbridge

Family

Family, I love family
Not all the time though
They're so annoying!
But they give you stuff:
Take mums for example
They're always moan, moan, moaning
But they give you stuff
And they take care of you
I'm stuck
I hate that word 'stuck'
It sounds like a slang word
I hate that word too
I'm not going to write 'I'm stuck' anymore
OK back to family treasures
I have a stepdad, stepsister, stepbrother, a mum and a pet cat
Their names are Ian, Alex, Max, Angie and Mitz
I'm stuck, *oh no!*
I love my pen
It's really nice because it's Winnie the Pooh and Piglet
I'm stuck
Argh! I hate that word!

Kelsey Cheadle (12)
Meole Brace School, Shrewsbury

Waterfall

W ater rushes down
A t me, I'm scared, no I'm
T errified, it's so fast
E ating away everything
R ushing at me, following me
F alling at me
A nd sends a shock wave up my spine
L ike a ripple going up me
L iving inside me is this waterfall.

Seb Adams (11)
Meole Brace School, Shrewsbury

Untitled

Do you know what it feels like to look at someone
Wanting them
But knowing that they will never be yours?
Wanting to be with them forever,
But knowing you can't.
You get this feelings when you see them,
Cannot be explained.
Feel empty when they are not around
What you feel for them never goes,
Instead it grows.
You try to think of other things,
Take your mind off them.
It doesn't work.
Permanent picture in your head
Of what it could be like.
Never going to happen though as much as you
Hope . . . dream . . . wish.
It hurts,
Feels like a thousand knives being stabbed in your heart
Yeah it hurts that much.
I'm stuck,
I don't know how to cope,
Because
The one thing I want
Is out of my reach.

Katie Fletcher (15)
Meole Brace School, Shrewsbury

My Thoughts

Ow! Eye hurts.
Don't know why, woke up with it.
I'm stuck.
Big dog! Small dog!
Those are my dogs. I have a big dog and a small dog.
I have fish, 13 of them.
I'm stuck.
I want to go home and fall asleep, *yawn.*
Mmm sleep.
Am I meant to write this?
Oh well, who cares.
I'm stuck.
Man I could eat a 12 inch Subway with olive, pepperoni,
Onion, tomato, lettuce, *mmm* and sweet onion sauce
And a chocolate cookie.
I'm stuck.
Still stuck.
I'm hungry and my eye hurts.
Don't know why.
I'm bored.
Only five hours to the end of school.
Aw man! Five hours.
Now I'm depressed.
Man am I bored.
Bored, bored, bored!

Rowan Lo (11)
Meole Brace School, Shrewsbury

I'm Stuck

Can you help me?
I'm split in two
I'm stuck
Stuck in a bottomless ditch
Which I can't get out of
No one else will help me
I'm stuck
Stuck in the middle
Someone tells me to do one thing
Another telling me to do the opposite
Being pushed around
Being an outsider
I'm sick
Sick of my life
Everyone else seems to be happier
Than me
I'm never happy
How I dream
Dream of feeling wanted
I'm stuck
How can I be seen?
I'm just invisible in the human eye
Just a speck
I'm stuck
I want to feel like a somebody
I want people to see me
For who I am
I'm stuck
And I can't get out.

Lizzie Stephens (15)
Meole Brace School, Shrewsbury

I'm Stuck

I'm in this English room
I'm stuck
I'm trapped
It's grey and dull outside, where's the sun in the sky?
I'm stuck
Wish I was at home not here
Anywhere but here
I'm bored
Too tired to concentrate
Words meaning nothing
Must pay attention
Need to pay attention
I'm stuck
So bored
Home time seems so far away
Time dragging on and on
It's so quiet in here
So dark outside
I'm trapped
Too tired to learn
Wish the work would go away
I have to learn, I must learn
Get good grades
I don't want to be stuck
Stuck in a dead-end job
Pressure, so much pressure
To do well
Succeed
Get the best in life
I'm stuck.

Sarah Carr (15)
Meole Brace School, Shrewsbury

Alone

Have you ever felt alone?
No family, no friends, no anyone
Going back to an empty home
If you can call this home

I'm stuck
Stuck in this life called Hell
I'm stuck
Walls closing in on me

Please help me
Please
I'm all alone
I'm scared

He's coming
I can hear him
The screams
I can't escape the screams

I must go
Go somewhere else, anywhere else
I must follow my heart away from here
I must . . .

He's still coming
Quick, escape while you still can
Run, I'll be OK.

Kim Williams (15)
Meole Brace School, Shrewsbury

Longing To Love You

I remember you Princess
How your eyes sparkled and shone
Your beautiful blonde hair blowing in the wind
I admired you
Always giving time to your brothers and sister
Staying up for a glimpse of the tooth fairy
The fatal day that you went
How you longed to be left
Alone. To play happily
'Eaten by animals'
Never!
Not even worth thinking about
We fought for you.
Never once being intimidated
By that monster.
Fighting, fighting, fighting,
Gone!
We got him darling
Never to be unleashed.

Here we are now
Longing to love you
Wishing, hoping, praying.
You're safe now, Child.
Up among the fairies
Laughing, playing
Your memory lives on Princess.

Rachel Barton (16)
Meole Brace School, Shrewsbury

My Free-Form Poem

I'm stuck
Same things over and over
It's things over and over
It's all maths
Even in science
Equilibrium?
In one ear, out the other
This is GCSE, what's A levels going to be like?
Coursework, mock exams, re-sits building
Pressure
I'm stuck, nothing new and interesting
Twenty past twelve, my only escape
Especially Friday - an afternoon of golf
I'm stuck
Head spinning, neck aching, work, work, work
Just want to go to sleep
I'm stuck . . . again.

Tom Jones (15)
Meole Brace School, Shrewsbury

English

I'm stuck,
I'm bored,
I hate this lesson, it's boring,
I feel thick, I'm stuck,
There's another forty minutes,
Feels like hours, like watching paint dry,
I'm stuck,
Nothing makes sense,
I shouldn't be here,
I hate it, I dread it,
I'm stuck
Make it fun,
Weather depressing, like this class
I'm stuck.

Abby Mills (15)
Meole Brace School, Shrewsbury

O' Sweet Child

I can remember you, O' sweet child!
As you took your first steps
Preparing to take on the world
Oh! Sweet joy you brought.

I can remember you, O' sweet child!
On your first day of school
As you sang and danced and played
Oh! What pride you brought.

I can remember you, O' sweet child!
On that day you first cycled
As the sun gleamed upon the frame
Oh! What a glorious day.

And now I see you laid before
Me for the last time
In a six foot box
Farewell!

Sophie Palmer (15)
Meole Brace School, Shrewsbury

My Sister

I think you're annoying, I think you're sad,
The grotesque feeling for you I once had.
We got into fights, you stole all my toys,
Between you and me, we didn't have joys.
You swung on your seat, fell off and blamed me,
You'd no idea how angry I would be.
But I'd hold it in, knowing something's true
I am your brother, I'll look after you.
Now we're grown up and I think you're alright,
I only show love now, no hate or spite.
So as we grow older from young to old,
Memories in mind will never be sold.
So yes we will die, but one thing remains,
The wonderful memories, in our brains.

Niall Hartshorn (16)
Meole Brace School, Shrewsbury

Schooldays

I go to school
Day after day
Week after week
It's so boring
I'm stuck
I want to go to sleep
I want to go home
I want doesn't get
I'm stuck
I look at the board
I don't understand a word
The teacher's shouting
Again
I'm stuck
I can't be bothered with this
Counting down the days until we leave
I can't wait
I'm stuck
I get my phone taken off me
Stupid teacher
Just because they ain't got any mates
I'm stuck.

Ashton Jones (15)
Meole Brace School, Shrewsbury

After The Earthquake

'Where are they?' I cried out,
Shifting bricks out of the way,
I searched through the rubble,
Desperately seeking my children,
Panic rushed through my body,
As I clambered, helpless with sadness.

I scrabble my way through,
Tears seeping down my face,
I call out my children's names,
But no answer.
'Help!' I cried to the rescuers,
I desperately wanted to find
My dear, beloved children.

Suddenly I shifted a rock,
There I saw a hand,
'Over here!' I yelled,
And they pulled my children out,
Great joy ran through my body
And tears ran down my face,
As I held my children in my arms
Safe, with no sound at all.

Amy Fletcher (12)
Meole Brace School, Shrewsbury

Fame

Take a magic Playboy bra,
Mix it up and it will go far,
Boil up with some lipstick,
Make sure it is very thick.

Take a pair of magic socks,
And cash will come in flocks.
Put in a new pink car,
And a bottle from a bar.

Boil it, fry it, blend to a tee
And you will be a celebrity.

Take a box of lipgloss,
Add a string of dental floss,
Fry it up with some Botox,
And you will be a sexy fox.

Last of all add some paint
And you will get a mate,
Drive around in a big pink car,
Up to an expensive bar.

Boil it, fry it, bend to a tee
And you will be a celebrity.

But after one whole year,
Your fame will disappear,
Try to get on with your life
And become a very good wife.

Naomi Wallace (14)
Meole Brace School, Shrewsbury

My Into The Future Poem

Into the future we go
Through thunder, rain, wind and snow
Melt the clock
To help time stop
Boil the potion
For slow motion

Mix and fry
To make us fly

Let's combine some rye
So we can be off and fly
Mix some snow to make us glow
Then we will be ready to go
A peck of this, a pinch of that
Then we will be out of here like that

Mix and fry
To make us fly

Into the future we go
Through thunder, rain, wind and snow
Hopefully we will make it
If we can bake it
If we add a pinch of hair
Maybe we will make it there

Mix and fry
To make us fly.

Naomi Morris (13)
Meole Brace School, Shrewsbury

The Invisible Potion

Add the cloak
Then begin to choke
Then peel a man's eye
That's clear to be a spy

To be invisible
You can't be civil

Then blend some vomit
Then combine a bomb that's atomic
Then add a spirit
And begin to skin it

To be invisible
You can't be civil

Then take a corpse that's stone dead
And mix it with a rat's head
Take the wing of a bird and roast
Then cook it with some toast

To be invisible
You can't be civil.

Ryan Sargeant (13)
Meole Brace School, Shrewsbury

Addicted

A ddicted to them,
D amaged by them,
D estroyed by them,
I solated,
C aptured with them,
T rapped with them,
E nvy from them,
D rugs is what they are.

Tom Reece (13)
Meole Brace School, Shrewsbury

Recipe For A Clown

Take a spoonful of laughter
Throw in a tub of grease paints
Put in some courage
Spoon in some guts
Put in some jokes
Fry in some clothes
Sprinkle some props
Slice in the circus
Cry in some tears
Place some food
Bake some hairy noses
And last of all
Some silly string
And there you have it
A clown.

Tom Colley (12)
Meole Brace School, Shrewsbury

Some Day My Brother

Oh! As the deafening machine beeps,
You lay quietly, as family weeps.
As your eyes are closed so peacefully, wake!
The atmosphere in the room: cruel, edgy, opaque.
As I look down to you with sorry rage
You always looked up to me whatever age.
Your eyes no longer sparkle like the sky's stars,
Your body covered in emotionless scars.
Your sun-bright smile shines no more, not of late,
Your mouth shut, like the doors of your unfair fate.
Mountainous, your soul will fly high if you sleep,
If you don't wake, in my heart you stay deep.
Some day, my brother, you will wake from your dreams,
Some day, my brother, you will wake from your dreams.

Eddy Key (15)
Meole Brace School, Shrewsbury

Emotions

Emotions, emotions, emotions
The fastest roller coaster around
The thoughts twist and turn
Round and round in my mind
I am a teenager
I shout and scream
And stamp my feet
When I am happy I don't think to cry
When I am crying I just want to die
I am stuck
One day you feel on top of the world
The next you feel
Just like you're a little girl
I feel so grown up, feel so tall
The world is so small to me
So little, so fragile
Boy, well that's what they think
Oh how so little, naive, so sweet
That's what everyone thinks
I am a teenager
I shout and scream and stamp my feet
I am stuck
So why am I aching like a baby?
Going all crazy like this
But am I proving my point?
If I am so grown up
Why am I stamping my feet?
I stamp louder and louder and louder
Harder and harder
The sound gets more and more
Till I slam my door and it's gone.

Kirsty Price (15)
Meole Brace School, Shrewsbury

Theseus And The Minotaur

My heart thumping,
The Minotaur's in my mind.
I'm sweating,
Tension in every drip.
Minotaur, here I come!

I open the door,
Rats everywhere.
My heart beats faster,
Echoing in the distance.
Guts, *err!*

A magic ball,
From Ariadne.
I clench my sword harder.
Following the weaving ball,
I can smell the Minotaur.

There's the Minoatur,
Eating at the human flesh.
I drop my sword,
He turns round,
Drops his meal and runs.

In and out,
I dodge and dodge.
Uh-oh, I'm cornered
He charges, and misses.
His horns get stuck and he's dead.

Dancing about, I've won!
I follow the string back.
Forget to bring Ariadne
Celebrate good times.

John Andrews (11)
Meole Brace School, Shrewsbury

A Week Of Summer Weather

On Monday the hot sun looked down
and people were complaining all over the town.

Tuesday was a better day,
but I suppose it could be hotter than May.

On Wednesday children were having treats,
but no one walked along our streets.

Thursday stood out warm and hot,
but the room was as hot as a pot.

Friday's sun was clear and calm,
the sun was paler than my arm.

Saturday's sky was blue and warm,
phew! It still felt like a boiled palm

Sunday started fairly grey,
still children were coming out to play.

Eve Edwards (12)
Meole Brace School, Shrewsbury

The Strongest Bond

The first vague memory of my brother.
In the hospital, held by my mother.
Early childhood together was blurred,
Memories of Christmas in the past stirred.
We were continuously in conflict,
Opinions and jealousy made us split,
But an overwhelming bond reined us in.
The family tree, brothers of a kin.
The family fruit didn't fall far apart.
This made the struggle a race to outsmart,
Each other, at the passions we shared in life,
The winner took glory, the loser strife,
But the bond ensured the sorrow was shared,
The strong bond of brotherhood will be tarred.

Josh Whittaker (15)
Meole Brace School, Shrewsbury

Divorce

I wasn't there. My conscious mind and eyes were flooded.
I was in the shadows.
The silver moon shone its soft glowing light upon the carpet before me.
Everything shimmered like a dream, but it wasn't a dream.
My inner senses were deranged.
I had a deep, dark, burning emptiness inside me.
As I sat, I rocked to my lullaby of slamming doors and screaming
voices.
I was a tear-drenched soul whose parents had ripped her in two.

I see now, it's not so bad living in two halves.
It still tears me apart, I am caught in the middle.
This is my pain, this burning hole, it's mine.
It hurts so much, it belongs to me.
But I see why now, you did it for me,
You did it for him, you did it for her.
And you did it for you.

Aby Edwards (15)
Meole Brace School, Shrewsbury

14th December

That morning *you'd* kissed me on the cheek,
Yesterday's eruption of temper now forgotten from our minds
And wished me a good day from the deep oceans of your eyes.
Coming out of school so early seemed foreign.
Arriving home to find the rooms full of river-eyed strangers and friends
And Mum sitting silent in *your* armchair, waiting to speak.
At 10-years-old my world crumbled cruelly around me.

Now, as the 14th of December steals up on us again,
The winter's wind will whip bitterly cold.
There will be nobody to warm me with a big bear hug.

Leanne Biggs (15)
Meole Brace School, Shrewsbury

Theseus And The Minotaur

Sailing from Athens.
A lump in our throats.
Across the sea to Crete.
Then, the island we approach.
So this is our fate.

Following the string.
A gift from Ariadne.
To aid our safe return.
I must keep it with me.
As my stomach starts to churn.

Inside the labyrinth.
It's musty, dark and damp.
I'm frightened to the core!
Onward through the cobwebs
Towards the Minotaur.

Facing the monster.
The hideous beast sleeps.
Half man and half bull.
Then I softly creep.
No more will his stomach be full.

Let battle commence.
I yelled and then charged.
I thrust my sword at his heads.
He slashed me then threw me.
But I strangled him dead.

Sailing to Athens.
Leaving Ariadne behind.
In my sadness there's no white sail.
So Father jumped from the cliffs
And I am a lonely ruler.

Georgina Evelyn Davies (11)
Meole Brace School, Shrewsbury

Theseus

Breathing becomes gasping,
Eyes become motionless,
Sweat becomes torrents,
Heat becomes intense,
Smell becomes putrid.

The tunnel widens,
Skulls become scarce,
Rocks become smooth,
Streams become rivers,
Dark becomes light.

The string snags,
A distant roar,
A skull crunches,
Stench of death,
Drip, drip, drip.

There it is,
Huge pure beast,
It turns around
Eyes of fire,
Born to kill.

Sword Vs horn,
Shield Vs skin,
Man Vs beast,
Blood flying,
It is gone.

Hope at last,
Following the string,
Thought of celebration
Out of the Labyrinth
And away home.

Thomas Endacott (11)
Meole Brace School, Shrewsbury

Theseus And The Minotaur

Try to tie the string
Can't, fingers too sweaty
Once, twice, finally tied
I start to walk
My legs nearly buckle underneath me

I'm terrified
I touch the wall
My arms recoil immediately
Water? No, definitely blood
The crunch of bones under my feet

A low growl behind me
I spin around; nothing
I turn back
I realise I've dropped the string!
I've just signed my death

I drop to the floor
Scramble around searching
Searching for the string
I feel something new
Not the path

I look up, bloodshot eyes
Look back at me
My sword in my hand
Strike up, a lucky strike
Straight through the heart, dead

I drag the body to a wall
Using it to climb up
I see the exit, running, jumping
From brick to brick
Through the exit, I'm safe.

Benjamin Geddes (11)
Meole Brace School, Shrewsbury

Theseus

My heart pounding,
My adrenalin pumping,
My armour fine,
My shield just divine,
Sword at the ready.

I start walking,
I hear no talking,
I hope no one's stalking.
I shouldn't worry,
No lightning's forking.

In the dark,
I follow the string,
Even through the Labyrinth,
What can the darkness bring?
I won't worry.

I spot him.
Sweaty chest
And hairy arms,
The Minotaur,
Bringer of evil.

Unsheath my sword,
Swipe it thoroughly,
Born to kill.
The blood spills,
The Minotaur dead.

The journey home,
I leave Ariadne,
The sails still black
Ageus falls back
Drowned alive.

Daniel Gilbert (11)
Meole Brace School, Shrewsbury

Theseus And The Minotaur

Adrenaline pumping fiercely,
Determined, confident, fearless.
My sword at the ready.
'Quiet, too quiet,' I said.
My mind playing tricks on me.

Damp, dark, cramped.
Blood splattered on the wall.
Rats scurrying along the floor.
Blood dripping, heart pumping.
His cries in the background.

Scared, frightened, petrified.
The sweat falls off my face.
Boom-boom my heart pumps.
Closer and closer I get.
He could be around the corner!

Bloodshot eyes.
I see the Minotaur.
His coat covered in blood.
Black, black teeth
One of his horns broke in half.

Growl, swing, growl,
Swing, swing, swing, stab, swing
I stab him, he bleeds
Stab him again, he falls to the floor
Then becomes dead.

Proud, happy, relieved
People won't get killed anymore.
Rats scattering, they eat the Minotaur
The string goes on.
Light at the end of the tunnel, I run and run.

Jay Hadley (12)
Meole Brace School, Shrewsbury

Theseus And The Minotaur

Unwilling, petrified, gasping
Sword scraping on the walls
Hand sweating while holding my sword,
Heart shaking all the walls
Shield slipping in my grasp.

Claustrophobic, freezing cold
Bones crunching underfoot
Hearing things, seeing things
The whip of tails
Rotten bodies full of maggots

Screaming, crying, tripping
My hands slip off the string
Fall over, fumble on the ground
My feet slip in the blood
Darkness strangling me

Terrible, giant, deadly
Bloodshot eyes in the gloom
Horns as sharp as my sword
Muscle, nothing but muscle
A jaw which could eat the world

Blood, roars, screams
Blood splattering the walls
A horn gashing my waist
I fall, it's on top of me
I plunge my sword into its neck

Falling, screaming, bleeding
I run, pulling at the string
Light, no my eyes are lying
I trip, oh my head.

Oliver Haines (11)
Meole Brace School, Shrewsbury

The Labyrinth

Breathing rapidly, worried
Heart bumping, faster
Checking I am ready
My shield ready to protect.

Drips of blood, smelling
Eyeballs everywhere and skeletons
Dead people's heads
Dead bodies so scary.

Echoing, someone screaming
The string glows
Showing me where to go
I'm scared, nearly getting there.

Breathing down my chin
A big monster
Strong and ugly
Looks really evil and tough.

I had my sword, sharp
I stalked the Minotaur
He finally was dead
I left him hanging.

A black sail was there
Could that mean someone's died?
It could be my dad
It could be my lover
And I finally become king.

Leonardo Silva (11)
Meole Brace School, Shrewsbury

Theseus And The Minotaur Getting Ready To Fight

Unwilling, petrified, gasping
His heart pounding in the darkness
His sword scraping across the wall
Practising my fighting skills
Shield there to protect.

Frozen in the dark, damp cave
Shivers as I'm as cold as ice
Cannot see, like a blind bat
Skeletons rotting in the dampness
The stench of death smelling.

I can hear someone screaming, an echo
Load of sweat coming off my face.
People dying and rotting in the darkness.
My feet shivering fiercely.

Shouting, screaming, crying in the darkness,
My hand slowly slipping of the string.
Falling over and smashing my head onto the floor.
My head bleeding fiercely.
I safely reach out for the piece of string.

Blood splattering up the wall.
The Minotaur's horns crushing my stomach.
He knocks my head on the floor.
Before I pounce my sword straight into his heart.
Then he slowly dies.

Jordan Hall (11)
Meole Brace School, Shrewsbury

Labyrinth

Adrenaline pumping fiercely,
Sweaty, shaking, afraid.
Preparing equipment,
Sword at the ready,
Unsure what to expect.

Dripping, slimy, damp walls,
The putrid stench of death.
Feet sounding out,
Sword scraping past,
Echoing into the gloom.

String leading on,
Right, left, right,
A far-off roar,
A warning, a threat,
Telling of things to come.

Monster appearing suddenly,
Sweat dripping off muscles.
Bloodshot eyes
And matted fur
Horns sharp, preparing to kill.

I swing my sword,
It flashes in the torch light.
Dodging its blows
I stab at its heart
With roars of anguish, it slumps.

String leads on out,
I run to keep up
And finally break
Through the hard wooden door
Victorious, triumphant, relieved.

Oliver Lane (11)
Meole Brace School, Shrewsbury

Theseus

Theseus so brave,
Going in the Labyrinth,
Fighting the mighty Minotaur
Afraid, afraid, afraid,
I'm ready to attack.

Theseus so brave,
With the magic string,
Feel brave, feel determined,
You're the one,
The only one.

Theseus so brave,
Other lives depend on you,
You're deadly when unleashed,
As you wander through the Labyrinth,
Here I come.

Theseus so brave,
Until you come across the Minotaur,
Its jaws as big as your head,
You're petrified it's coming,
There's nowhere to run.

Theseus so brave,
The time has come,
The beast will die,
The beast pounces and you hit
He is down, he is dead.

Theseus so brave,
A hero, he's done it,
No more worries, just relief,
But you can't think what you've forgot,
Noooooooooooo, he's dead.

Lucy Lewis (11)
Meole Brace School, Shrewsbury

Theseus

Can't think properly,
Hands sweating like rivers,
Shuffling slowly forward,
Hands tighten on sword,
Really can't go on.

Walls crumbling, damp
Corpses rotting everywhere,
Rats creeping about,
Death all around,
Can't go back.

Bright, thread, light,
Could lead somewhere else,
Sometimes I lose it,
Maybe it might work,
Stumbling, can't go further.

Huge, monstrous thing,
Snorting and grumbling,
Muscles and veins bulging,
Blood splattered everywhere,
I'm frozen still.

We walk forward,
Sword clashes on claws,
I know what to do,
Blood splatters everywhere,
I leave him dead.

Boarding the boat,
Cold, harsh nights
Sea tossing us about,
Wet, rotting ship,
A screaming figure falls.

Jennifer Morgan (11)
Meole Brace School, Shrewsbury

Labyrinth

Heart pounding faster
Every shadow an enemy
Hands shaking with fear
Breathing, gasping in and out
Only seeing what is right.

Walking slowly, stealthily
Over moving carpets of rats
Bodies littering the floor
Stench of death always near
The sound of fate ringing.

As he follows
Hopes become lies
Following a ball of string
He starts to pray to the gods
For his fate lies within.

A sudden movement
The Minotaur has woken
Bloodshot eyes staring angrily
Teeth baring, jaggedly sharp
Beginning to charge.

Drawing his sword
Theseus fights back
Horn against sword
Finally the sword is encased
The Minotaur is no more.

Body exhausted completely
Sailing home with black sails
Forgetting those fateful words,
'Come back with white.'
Returning home to no father.

Jake Rainbow (11)
Meole Brace School, Shrewsbury

Labyrinth

Heart pounding, frightened,
Can barely breathe,
Confident, nervous, hopeful,
Sword out ready to fight,
Shield there to protect me.

Cold, damp, dripping,
Pictures on the wall,
Horrible smell and narrow,
Blood, people lying dead.

Thin, delicate, magical,
Will the magic work?
It's my lifeline
My leader to the Minotaur
My life depends on the string.

Gigantic, frightening, glaring,
Claws sharp, snorting, huge horns,
Terrified, fierce, bigger than anything else,
Hairy, ugly, big feet,
Horrible, scary, smelly.

Hard, fierce, sweating,
Sword slashing, shield bumping,
Charging, holding, beating,
Straining, throttling, smashing,
Aggressive, violent, bashing.

Victory, relaxing, finished,
Sealife, cool, wind,
Heart normal, glad, won it,
Father will be pleased, Theseus pleased,
Joyful, happy, fulfilled.

Collette Riggs (11)
Meole Brace School, Shrewsbury

Labyrinth

Hands clench hard
Sweat drips out of every pore,
Sword sharp and steely
Killing in my mind
Walls surround me, pushing in.

Darkness surrounds me,
Hopeful; am I going to live?
Palms grip the walls
Stench of blood lingers
Bodies grope at me!

I must follow,
A white ball of horsehair,
Rolling towards doom
I watch it glow
I follow its path.

A horned head
Spit drips to the floor
Its bloodshot eyes see
Its foul mouth eats
I'm spotted, fight.

Sword slashes,
Horns gouge
Necks crack
Arms broken
Dead is the beast.

Sailing home
Black sails raised
Figure on cliff falling
Falling, falling
Death engulfs him like water.

Samuel Rintoul (11)
Meole Brace School, Shrewsbury

The Journey Of The Labyrinth

My heart was pounding faster than a cheetah's
My lion chest was roaring, it was all smelly
There were rats underneath my nose
I kept looking over my shoulder to see if the Minotaur was behind me
Ready to eat me
I didn't want that to happen to me
I wanted to kill him once and for all.

I had had enough of this Minotaur
So it was time to take revenge
I felt a bit frightened, not really used to the dark.
I saw a tatty curtain and went inside
I saw the Minotaur, he was eating his prey.
I tiptoed and kicked a stone
The Minotaur heard me and kicked the stone back.
He turned and saw me and ran to me with his mouth open
It was dribbling.
I leapt out of his way, he turned and ran back to me
I held my sword out and stabbed it right in his heart.
Then I left his cave dead and silent
Walking down with my sword scraping on the ground.

Jodie Smith (11)
Meole Brace School, Shrewsbury

A Recipe For A Perfect Head Teacher

Take a spoonful of brown hair and two blue eyes,
Stir in a pinch of smiley faces,
Sprinkle in ten vendors, no vegetables forever,
Take a slice of games and listening to music,
Add roast credit awards, maybe nine or ten.
Grill some jeans, T-shirts and trainers,
So no school uniform forever.
Leave out schoolwork and seating plans,
Drop in caramels to eat in class,
Then, leave for two days and you will have a perfect head teacher.

Lisa Clarke (12)
Meole Brace School, Shrewsbury

Poem

You have my back
You hold my head
You are there for me to cry on
Spilling wet, salted tears into your softness
You let me release all my anger upon you
My blows feel only to you as feather on feather
When I undress you do not look away
I do not mind this though
I would find it strange if you did not watch
As I listen to music, you sit in deaf peace
As I write, you watch in blind darkness
As I talk, you relax in muted silence
As I touch and kiss, you remain unmoving in a crippled stupor
You are what I wake up to in the morning
And what I fall asleep next to at night
Thank you for your unquestioning love
Thank you for being there for me
Thank you for being my goosedown pillow.

Mike André (16)
Meole Brace School, Shrewsbury

D-Day

The smoke was as black as a midnight sky,
The bullets were like stars,
The bloodstained sand
Was as red as the English rose.

Relentless fire held us back,
But eventually we took hold.
Many died on that day,
But few of them were foes.

We buried our family,
We buried our friends,
But we can never bury the thoughts.

Tom Ashton (13)
Meole Brace School, Shrewsbury

He Stabbed Me!

Where am I?
It's so dark,
Anybody there?
I'm all alone!

It's so cold,
Wait, I'm outside,
The night sky's pitch-black,
Where is everyone?

I'm stuck, I'm lost,
I've got to get out,
But how?
A shudder runs down my spine!

What's that noise?
I'm being followed
I'm running,
But not moving.

He's getting closer
Help! Anyone!
His hand's on my shoulder
He's got something.

He's jabbing me with it.
It's a knife. What does he want?
It must be a dream
Wake up! Wake up!

He stabbed me
I'm awake, what a twisted dream!
What's this? It's blood!
There's a black figure by the window.
Ashes to ashes, dust to dust!
He stabbed me.

Sarah Campbell (14)
Meole Brace School, Shrewsbury

Dad

It was a cold day,
The day that you left.
Packing your bags,
To load up your car.
With a mattress on the roof
And the boot full up.
It was all she had left you with,
After twenty years of marriage.
I cried that day,
As you drove away.
Ripped from my life.
I couldn't blame you:
You had done no wrong.
I was sure it was the end of the world,
My young life so torn apart.

Now I can visit you
And I do every weekend.
The highlight of my broken week
And then I can see you.
We can sit and talk for hours,
'How was your week?'
But our time together is short-lived,
As I'm taken from you on Sunday evening.
Once again my life is torn open,
As I'm driven back home.
Only to wait another week,
Until the weekend comes back around.

For me to be broken once again.
Torn, ripped and slashed.

Callum Onions (15)
Meole Brace School, Shrewsbury

Malignant

I seem to recall the first time we met,
The world was still new and clean.
We were ready to work at our love
Even though it would struggle
Silently while I wept.
I seem to recall the second time we met,
You took me into your soft grip.
While others looked on in jealous hatred
Across pale, peeling files that tore me up,
Just as they ravaged your world.

I seem to recall the third time we saw,
I walk across to your open side.
The pulsating carcass screams within me
While the heat burns all knowledge of my tailored world
As you guide me in further and further.
I seem to recall the last time we met,
I see the way your shadow-strained eyes burn into mine.
As the terminal reality rages and spreads
Through your body, my hand reaches out
And finds your empty space.

Nadine Loach (15)
Meole Brace School, Shrewsbury

Untitled

Grandfather you used to be so wise
Evil alcohol enveloped you and all the good times
You come to visit for your Sunday roast
Alcohol didn't mean so much back then.
I used to look up to you as a friend
Every Sunday you would turn up when due
To entertain us with stories that you knew
You would sit at the table with your drink
Little did you know it would be the end of you.

Now it's too late to change your ways
People come to visit you at your grave
They look back at all the good times
Now on a Sunday we sit down to eat
Full of boredom as you're not here to speak.
If you had just taken a little more care
You would have lived a lot longer than you think
Mealtimes on a Sunday aren't the same
We don't always sit together to eat
Instead we go out and eat when we please
Sundays used to be a family time
Not any more, you took that with you when you went away.

Jason Blakemore (15)
Meole Brace School, Shrewsbury

Admiration

Without you I would be nothing
Like a flower without the sun's fiery heart.
You were always there for me
Something I could lean towards
Giving me extra energy.
Your flickering presence never failed to astound me,
As I watched upon you when you weren't aware.
The colours you created in my world
Were as beautiful as a blossoming bud.
Through the heat and pain
Of leading two separate lives,
I never doubted you, though it may not have seemed.

Now I have to live for the future,
Look ahead and be the same,
As you once taught me and I'll never forget,
The power of fiery flames concerning passion for one,
Or the defiant lifelong embers
That will make me grow like you.
No matter what the moment extinguishes
There is a lick of hope,
A trailing leaf of love
That will make me think of you.

I know you will always be there for me.

Daniela Baur (15)
Meole Brace School, Shrewsbury

Nonsense Poem

It was like when you'd been searching all night,
Then you get a fright,
All through the night,
I'm stuck, I'm stuck,
Then a frog came out
And made me shout out,
'Oh my God, it's a frog!'

Then I ran into the night
Got another fright
It was a scream,
A blackening, blood-curdling, ear-piercing scream
That sent shivers up my back.

I am stuck like glue on paper
I am stuck, I am stuck.
'Hello, are you home?'
I want to escape this place
This terrible place.
It was like trying to escape from a metal box
That had a padlock on the outside, but the key was within,
I am stuck in a swamp full of crocodiles and smelly flowers
Which get up my nose and I sneeze so loud I'm in China,
With a dragon who has a twisted face and nostrils the size of
                                                    dinner plates.

Mark Beale (12)
Meole Brace School, Shrewsbury

An Eternal Sleep

Since that sorrowful day,
When I crouched on the stairs.
When my father had a phone call.

I burst into tears, when I was told.
I sat in my bed for hours crying.
Sitting upright, remembering the last time we met.

I dressed in black, my mother helping me
And walked slowly to the car,
Following a suited man in a sombre march.

Seeing the people, waiting outside the church,
Waiting for us, relatives I had never seen before.
People I had never seen before, friends of the deceased.

I went in, feeling nothing, past the benches to the front row,
Six people marched in holding the coffin,
In an eternal sleep.

Never to wake.
He did have a full life,
The fullest I had ever seen.

I now sit here writing this poem
The last present he ever gave me
Above on my shelf.

I know where you are, under the great oak tree,
Never been there since I was ten.
I still look at photos and remember that I remain.

Hanne Thorpe (16)
Meole Brace School, Shrewsbury

Cinderella

Cinderella was fed up and sad
She was made to do all of the work
Some of it was very bad
Then her stepmum deserted her

Cinderella is very nice, but
She had to live with mice
She is very pretty
And sings a pretty ditty

Cinders has to clean the chimney black
Some parts are very bad
One time she hurt her back
That made her very sad

The two ugly sisters were very cruel
They made her do all of the work
And made her look a fool
Overall they were very nasty

The fairy godmother did some magic
So Cinderella could go to the ball
But something happened that was very tragic
The prince didn't like her at all

Cinderella had a broken heart
And looked like a fool
The mother did it all herself
That was very cruel.

Rebecca Dowley (13)
Meole Brace School, Shrewsbury

Battered And Bruised

My heart is in my mouth, I cannot move
My son is buried beneath brick and rocks
I feel the earth shaking and shattering two more times.

I could not speak
I could not cry
I could not weep
I didn't know why.

A sudden move would take his life
Only if I am steady will he have a chance
Take too long he will fall into darkness
I moved the rocks above him but I heard no cry.

I gently blew clouds of dust from his face
His eyes opened like a newborn baby
My son who was minutes from death
Lay battered and bruised in my arms.

He did not speak
He did not move
He just laid there
Battered and bruised.

Rhys Roser (12)
Meole Brace School, Shrewsbury

A Recipe For An Alien

Give an injection of ferret's energy,
Drop in a crocodile's tail,
Add one bug's eye with X-ray powers,
Wind round one set of octopus' tentacles,
Stir with one iron foot,
A rabbit's whisker,
Put them all on a hippo's body.

James Evans (13)
Meole Brace School, Shrewsbury

Invisibility

Invisibility's a magic thing,
mix it up while you sing,
add it in your own time,
mix it up while you mime.

Mix and stir all day long,
do it with a playful song.

Why not add some fairy dust,
add it with a very cold gust,
add some blue window glass,
more and more what a mass.

Mix and stir all day long,
do it with a playful song.

Add some clouds from up high,
right up there in the sky,
not a sound, not even a squeak,
now more ingredients you must seek.

Mix and stir all day long,
do it with a playful song.

Cut up parts of a cloak,
then you hear a funny old croak,
hunt it down poor old frog,
in it goes with a scatter of fog.

Mix and stir all day long,
do it with a playful song.

Now your mixture is complete,
put it on to the heat,
wait until it starts to simmer,
then you eat and start to shimmer.

Mix and stir all day long,
do it with a playful song.

Joanne Hockenhull (13)
Meole Brace School, Shrewsbury

The Prey That Got Away

It was like when you have been searching all night,
I have been searching all night.
The prey I so badly needed for energy was in my grasp.

I lowered myself to the ground, adrenaline in my blood,
My four feet flew off the ground
And my teeth clamped into my prey.

I tasted the blood in my mouth as the predator came out of me,
In my sudden rush of adrenalin and energy
I never noticed the prey pull apart my jaws and run.

Did this creature so low in the food chain
Even realise who I am?
I let out a mighty howl as if to say, 'Bring it on.'

I chased and chased until my feet had other ideas,
I pressed on watching my paws fly over branches and such,
My head flew high to see a weapon,
This weapon appeared to be death.

Bang!

The prey I so badly needed for energy had become predator,
This wasn't fair.
Two-legged creatures take my food and now my life,
As for me, this was the prey that got away . . .

Stephanie Cochran (13)
Meole Brace School, Shrewsbury

The Three Little Pigs

'I will huff and I will puff and I will blow your house down.'

The three little pigs leave home,
Their mum now leaves them alone.
The wolf will huff and puff.
For the pigs things will be tough.

'I will huff and I will puff and I will blow your house down.'

The first little pig builds a house of straw.
He's proud of his home and he's pleased with his work.
And he watches TV and goes to sleep.

'I will huff and I will puff and I will blow your house in.'

The second little pig builds a house of sticks.
He's really chuffed with his home.
But the wolf turns up and knocks on the door.
Then he eats the pig up in his turn.

'I will huff and I will puff and I will blow your house in.'

The third little pig builds a house of bricks.
He's really happy he lives alone.
But the wolf comes back with a gun and a cap.
Then he huffs and puffs and shoots the pig down.

'I will huff and I will puff and I will blow your house in.'

Sophie Cooper (12)
Meole Brace School, Shrewsbury

Cinderella

Cinderella's mum died, she was sad
Her stepmum made her hide
Her stepmum made her clean
Cinderella was never seen.

A letter came from the ball
Cinderella couldn't go at all
Cinderella's godmother came
And said that wasn't a bother.

Fairy godmother was very good
A pumpkin turned to wood
The horses were very nice
They were hungry like mice.

Cinderella goes to the ball
She didn't like what she saw at all.
Her ugly sister was dancing with the prince
It made her wince.

Cinderella and her sister had a fight
With all their might
The other one hit her on the head
Now Cinderella is dead.

Dan Pryce (12)
Meole Brace School, Shrewsbury

Billy Goats Gruff

'I will go over the bridge
Into the field of grass
So tall and nothing to hurt me
But I will not eat it all fast.'

'Who's that trampling over my bridge?
You look nice, so I'll eat you.'
Crunch, chew, crunch, chew,
'That's my snack today.'

'I will go over the bridge
Into the field of grass
So tall and nothing to hurt me
But I might eat all the grass.'

'I will go over the bridge
Into the field of grass
So tall and nothing to hurt me
I will eat all the grass.'

'No more goats will eat
This grass ever again
Ha, ha, ha, ha, ha, ha, ha, ha!'

Thomas Fewtrell (12)
Meole Brace School, Shrewsbury

Three Little Pigs

Three little pigs were chased by a wolf
The wolf ran in his house
The wolf he ran away
The pigs sat as quiet as a mouse

He left his mum's home
And built a house of straw
But the house that wolf had blown
Didn't have a front door

His house was built of sticks
He worked very hard
The wolf was up to his tricks
And blew that house down

The last pig was very clever
He made his of bricks
He never thought he would blow it down ever
The wolf was up to his old tricks

The wolf planted some dynamite
The house he was going to blow
He lit it with all his might
For the pigs there will be no tomorrow

The pigs were dead
There were lots of guts
Wolf chopped off the heads
Then there were no huts.

Kieran Boyes (12)
Meole Brace School, Shrewsbury

I Don't Know What To Write

I'd like to write a poem
Or even write a rap.
I write on the stairs,
I write in the car,
Even though it's not for me,
I don't really care.
Sometimes I get really stuck,
I look up at the blue sky,
It gives me inspiration for the poem I call,
'I Can't Think What to Write'.

I rap along the railings,
I rap all day and night,
Even though it gets on my friends' nerves,
I squeal like a cat.
I can't think what to write
For this rap, thingy type poem
Called, 'I Can't Think What to Write'.

I rap along the tightrope,
I can't think what to write.
I know cos guess who's back with a new rap
Called, 'I Don't Know What to Write'?
Please help me as it nears half two,
For the lesson I dread,
Is coming nearer.
I have to hand in this poem
Called, 'I Don't Know What to Write'.

Nathan Hinks (12)
Meole Brace School, Shrewsbury

As Day Turns To Night

It was like when you have been,
Searching, all the night.
The clouds up above,
Blocking out the stars
And I am stuck, stuck!
The moon lights up the night sky,
As it passes through the night.
Black as the sky was
I could still see perfectly clear.

The day came and the sun was clear and bright
And I don't know what to say,
It's like I am as dumb as a twig
Lying there all alone.

Dusk,
The sky changes colour,
Yet again.
It's like I am moving from one scene to another in a film.
But it's unclear,
As I don't know what to say.
Being stuck doesn't help,
At about 8 o'clock at night.
The stars soon to be out
When day turns to night.

Gemma Almond (12)
Meole Brace School, Shrewsbury

Live Forever, Eternal Life

A thickened everlasting heart,
Simmered with a year that never parts,
Bubble up anti-ageing,
My whole life I can be saving.

Slice and boil a stopped clock,
Then healthy bones that never rot.

Roast and braise a baby turtle,
Then stir my potion in a circle,
Brew up a treasured fossil
And a whale that is colossal.

Slice and boil a stopped clock,
Then healthy bones that never rot.

Steam some lungs,
That will never be hung,
Then simmer a pair of eyes,
They're always sure to be wise.

Slice and boil a stopped clock,
Then healthy bones that never rot.

Stew some tinted new ears,
Then hear them out, without fears,
Grate some fair hair,
That is held with lots of care.

Sally Odell (13)
Meole Brace School, Shrewsbury

Runaway Mum

My mother used to be my idol,
I wanted to be just like her,
She would always have a happy face, so would I.
She didn't have one bad bone in her body,
I thought she was my best friend, I was hers,
I knew she would always be there for me,
One day I came home and Mum wasn't there,
I waited anxiously for hours - still no Mum.

I've moved on since that day,
I no longer see what I thought was Mum's smile,
But I share the grimace that was stuck on her face.
I was right, she didn't have one bad bone in her body,
They were all that way,
Mum wasn't there for me anymore,
I don't want to be like her,
She crushed my trust, life and happiness.
What I wanted to be like was all a deceitful act.
Mum left us when I was 10,
She's started a new family.

Alice Wheeler (15)
Meole Brace School, Shrewsbury

Recipe For A Dragon

Take a spoonful of a venomous snake's fangs,
A pack of matchsticks,
Sprinkle with power and a bull's horn,
Wings of a bat,
Tail of a lizard,
Stir it up with tongue of a snake,
Scales of a rat,
Ears of a horse,
Spikes of a crocodile,
Shake it up with
Eyes of an evil witch,
And most of all swirl it up with rabbits' feet.

Alex Tovey (12)
Meole Brace School, Shrewsbury

Untitled

It was like you've been searching all night,
When the moon and stars burn and bite.
Your neck emblazoned,
With the shadows and shine, gold.
Blue, green, the colours of the eyes
Like the people who left before you,
Down the valley of no return.
Well, they returned
And the valley vanished,
Escaping like a man on the run.
It was like the first,
Last and afterwards
And in the hedgerows of Albion,
With its satellite towns
And the twisted hazel trees,
They helter-skelter for eternity.

James Hickson (15)
Meole Brace School, Shrewsbury

A Recipe For An Evil Teacher

Take a black book and detentions,
Homework all the time
And after school every night.
Add a sprinkle of bad fashion sense,
Simmer and boil.
Add black eyes
And purple cabbage for hair.
She makes you eat cabbage all the time,
Bans sweets.
She will live in the school basement with a rat as her pet.
The skeleton of her husband in the cupboard.
Now you have the world's most evil teacher!
Nooooo!

Natalie Brookes (12)
Meole Brace School, Shrewsbury

Cinderella

A beautiful princess, Cinderella
Lived with her stepmother in slavery,
Her two ugly sisters of her beauty
Were filled with jealousy.

One day came a letter from the prince
Inviting them to a ball,
Cinderella begged to go
But her mother didn't say yes at all.

Cinderella sat weeping on the ground
Feeling lonely and sad.
'What has happened?' said her fairy godmother.
Cinderella said, 'I'm treated really bad.'

She changed the mice into horses
Using her impressive magic,
She changed the frog into a coach,
Cinderella's life will no more be tragic.

She also warned her
Before the clock beats twelve,
For all shall go
Exactly at twelve.

She went to the ball
All beautiful and nice.
Her sisters shot her saying,
'You should have thought twice!'

Nahla Safwat Ashour (13)
Meole Brace School, Shrewsbury

5 Minutes Of Random Confusion

It was like when you have been searching all night,
Searching, searching in the dark,
Up, down, left, right,
And I still don't know what I'm looking for.
It is confusing.
I don't like Barbies, they are annoying,
What with the pink clothes (I don't like pink), cheesy smile,
Plastic bendy arms,
They are annoying. Very.
But I do like pigs, even though half the time they're pink as well.
But then they can be brown, brown, brown as mud.
Pigs are cool.
My name is Tim Farrow.
Hasn't changed.
Still Tim.
Yeah, Tim all the way till four o'clock, on film, yeah
And I am proud to say that I have never had any desire
To be called Cecil.
I wish I was called Cecil.
No I don't.
I don't know.
Oh well.
This is Tim Farrow,
Signing out from
Nowhere.

Tim Farrow (12)
Meole Brace School, Shrewsbury

5 Minute Poem

It was like when you have been searching all the night,
I can still hear his little squeaky bark.
When I saw his basket and he wasn't there,
It gave me a fright.
His little red ball was still there,
I searched the house from top to bottom,
Looking in every room and cupboard
But I had no luck,
All I found was his little winter coat made of cotton.

It was like searching for nothing,
I knew he wasn't in the house but I kept looking,
I then saw his photograph on the fireplace.
I then realised that I had to tell my mum,
Who was cooking.
She rang up the local kennels and told them what had happened.

That was 5 years ago and I've had no luck,
But I can still hear his little squeaky bark.

Sian Owen (12)
Meole Brace School, Shrewsbury

My Wonderful Place

There is a place, a most wonderful place,
Where the hot summer day is not a race.
Where the sharp grains of sand are a golden brown
And this place is far away from a busy town.
The sea is a glistening tropical blue
And all you can hear is distant cows moo.
The towering cliffs behind the small beach
Only make it accessible from the boat's reach.
There is the occasional seagull's cry,
As it circles round into view of the eye.
Black heads pop up close to the beach's shore,
Silent and still is the seal, not like a lion's roar
And this small place, is a most wonderful place,
Where the hot summer day is not a race.

Rebecca Griffiths (12)
Meole Brace School, Shrewsbury

One Night In Istanbul

With seas of red
And a pitch of green,
The greatest match the world has seen.

As the tension builds throughout the stands
The match begins,
Liverpool Vs Milan.

With seconds gone
The Reds are down,
Rafa Benitez forced to frown.

Half-time,
The score is three,
Game over, so it would seem.

It's not over yet for the mighty Reds,
They've got a goal back
From Steven Gerrard's head.

With another two goals,
The score at 3-3.
The match shall be decided on penalties.

The first penalty
Against AC Milan,
Was scored by Mr Didi Hamann.

With Liverpool ahead and Shevchenco up next,
It was all up to Dudek
To save Liverpool's necks.

Breaths held and eyes shut,
None dared to watch
As the kick was took.

A dive to his right, a hand held high,
The kick was saved!
Milan did sigh.

Champions of Europe!
That is no lie,
And thinking about that night in Istanbul
Still brings a tear to my eye.

Ed Morrell (14)
Meole Brace School, Shrewsbury

My Forgetful Potion

In I throw a turtle shell,
That makes the ringing of a bell.
Then I boil a fish's brain,
To make my foe dull and lame.
1, 2, 3 in goes part of my potion,
That adds to part of the commotion.
Washing powder goes on in,
To make my enemy's brain dull and dim.
This chant I've made is oh so good,
It will make my foe as thick as wood.
1, 2, 3 in goes part of my potion,
That adds to part of the commotion.
What now will I add to my plan?
I know, I'll add chemical X,
That I also call Tipp-ex.
1, 2, 3 in goes part of my potion,
That will add to the commotion.
Now to end my perfect charm,
I stir my potion with a zombie's arm.

Michael Fennell (13)
Meole Brace School, Shrewsbury

The Little Butterfly

The
little
butterfly
fluttering by
is gold, red and green.
It stops dead still,
wings sway slow.
Fly away
now!

Becky Winwood (13)
Meole Brace School, Shrewsbury

Too Sick!

I can't go to school today
I'm feeling rather ill.
My nose is hanging from my face,
My heart is going at a pace.
I've got the measles and the mumps,
My hair is coming out in clumps.
My head is sore,
There's a pain in my jaw.

I have been sick,
Just really quick.
Oh please, oh please
My snot is green when I sneeze.
My arms are broke,
If I eat I will choke.
I can't go to school today
I'm too sick!
Wait a tick . . .
Isn't it a holiday?
Wahey!

Elsie Cinnamond (12)
Meole Brace School, Shrewsbury

Evil Teacher

One fat nose
And X-ray eyes.
Add a spoonful of hate,
Add two Devil's horns
And six vampire teeth.
Wrap around long red hair.

Add daily detentions
And after schools too.
He gives you homework every night,
You can't sit next to who you want.

Ross O'Callaghan (12)
Meole Brace School, Shrewsbury

5 Minute Poem

It is like I've been searching
All night wondering what to do.
Nothing is in my head,
I've just gone blank.
Oh, I've got it,
Colours, don't you just love them?
Red and yellow,
Pink, err, that ain't a nice colour.
Orange, blue, I love them
And I love Leeds
They're the best.
Blue and yellow
And Celtic
Green and white,
They kick ass.
I love colours, they mean loads,
Imagine no colours
That would be cool but
That would mean no
Chanting my favourite chant . . .
Fly the flag, it's blue and amber,
Imagine.

Ailsa Young (12)
Meole Brace School, Shrewsbury

The X Factor

Sitting in the waiting room,
Waiting to be called,
Sweat is upon the brow
And you wait to be called.

At last a call, 'Next,'
And you are in,
Three solemn faces
Stare back from the din.

Your stomach churns nervously,
Your heart misses a beat,
You shuffle slightly on your weakening feet
And remember that you are there to sing.

Then your mouth opens to sing,
You sing as you know how,
You finish your memorised song
And give a little bow.

The verdict is taken,
You are through to the next round.
You leap up happily from the cold, hard ground
And you shout out loudly with a happy grin,
'I've got the X factor!'

Gemma Cusack (14)
Meole Brace School, Shrewsbury

A Father's Sorrow

Gently in a soothing voice I ask,
'Angela are you there?'
Hearing nothing I tell her not to worry,
Crying in sadness, in sorrow,
'She's alive,' I tell myself not believing it.

Scrabbling and scratching away carefully,
Pulling rock away from her possibly dead body.
As slowly as I can I study the rocks,
Hoping against hope to find her alive,
Listening to hear her delicate voice.

A finger - just a finger but her finger,
I pull her out, crying in joy.
My sorrow gone, my words catching in my throat,
I have pulled her away from Death's grasp,
The Grim Reaper can have her no more.

Jessica Morgan (12)
Meole Brace School, Shrewsbury

The Hunt

It was like when you have been searching all night,
Tracking the wolf through the wood,
Filled with revenge for the many that lay dead on its soul.

Still searching
The black of its eyes,
The red of bloodstained teeth.

All the while looking like a clown
In front of the forest,
As I'm tracking it laughs at the way I move.

The beast as quiet as night,
Running from the hunters,
The twisted beast bent on evil was getting away,
And our vengeance won't be filled.

William Royle (13)
Meole Brace School, Shrewsbury

Help, Get Me Out Of Here

I'm stuck in a room filled with evil,
There is no love in this awful place.
I would love to see my family so much,
But I can't get out of this place.
I have not yet found a door, which they said I would find.
They lied, they lied. How can it be?
Why, why was it that they lied to me?
If I will ever get out of this place
I will find the nearest phone,
I will ring my parents, I will run home.
I will never be alone.
I will hold someone close to me for all eternity
And not let go till my time,
Time has come to go and live in Heaven,
With all the peace in the world.
But here in this dark place, underground, I am stuck,
Pleading helplessly with all the words in my heart,
'Help, get me out of here!'

Tracy Stott (12)
Meole Brace School, Shrewsbury

The Wind Singer

As I march my voice grows strong,
Stronger than the birds of wolves.
My sword glints from the light of the sun,
Of the power of the Morah,
For we are his men, his army,
We are the Zars.
Let us not fear, let others fear before us.
Now we march to our tuneless song,
The only word is 'kill'.

Gary Smith (12)
Meole Brace School, Shrewsbury

One Death In War

It was like when you have been searching all night,
Bang!
First shot fired, we'd found it,
'Move in!'
I raised my gun to the window,
I pull the trigger, he falls to the floor,
That didn't feel good,
Red drips from the window.

Front door flies open,
Room is full of them, *'Fire!'*
Clown on TV shatters with the bullets,
Four left I think.
He fired, my gun drops
Like a child, in a crowd, I fell.

Quiet now, so quiet,
I see my commander stare blankly down at me,
My twisted body, peacefully on the floor, think, think . . .
It's over,
I smile,
This is what it feels like,
Whiteness.

Owen Kelly (14)
Meole Brace School, Shrewsbury

Red Mist

It was like when you have been searching all night,
So bad the feeling that you need to run,
Wherever, whenever,
The red mist sinks on to you
And when it sinks,
You feel depressed.
Because you feel like that,
Like you're at the bottom of the sea.

It's like you're in a circus
And you've made a big mistake,
Your face is really red
As you hear the clocks go gong.

It strikes 5 o'clock
And the red mist
Sinks again,
But this time it sinks forever,
Never to be moved
And it sinks when it's so thick
That it almost blinds your eyes.
It does what other mists can't do,
So be careful,
It could kill you.

Lyle Sambrook (12)
Meole Brace School, Shrewsbury

What Happened?

It was like when you have been searching all night for the answer,
So what do I do now?

I have a feeling I have lost something special
And where have all the colours gone?
All there is to see is grey,
Just grey, dull and very boring.

What is happening? I feel so strange.
I hear music like when they're doing tricks at a circus
And they're laughing,
But it feels as though they're laughing at me.

Am I dreaming or what?
I don't seem to be waking up,
Time to panic,
It is like I'm going mad, but I'm not,
I know I'm not.
What is happening?

It's all strange and twisted,
I can't work out where I am
Or what is going on around me.
I feel lonely, very lonely . . .
Help! Somebody help!
But there is no one, I don't like it.
Stop it, stop it! Let me out,
I want to scream and be free.
I want to see my family, my friends,
But I can't and I'm scared,
So I sit and wait . . . and wait . . . and wait
But what's the use? There is nothing!

Siân Lloyd (13)
Meole Brace School, Shrewsbury

The Soldier

Heart pounding faster and faster,
His sword ready to fight,
Waiting for the fight to arrive,
Scared out of his skin,
Brave to beat the enemies,
Determined to have courage.

Scared of what's going to happen,
He puts on an evil face
Knowing that he is petrified,
Ready to beat the enemies,
Bloodshot eyes wanting to cry,
Thinking, *I can't cry, have some courage.*

The fight commences,
Gory as you can imagine,
Swords flying everywhere,
Blood shot across the ground,
True bravery would be needed
In the dampness of the sky.

People shouting,
Puddles of blood lay on the ground.
Soldiers staring at the victims,
Competitive soldiers fighting,
Soldiers fighting for their families,
Hundreds of people on the ground.

The fight is now over,
The brave soldier's won.
No more chaotic shouting,
He's home safe and sound,
No more worrying, love is all around him.

Charlie Louise Davidson (11)
Meole Brace School, Shrewsbury

Carnage

The time of year was right
For the crazed psychopaths
Let out to fight,
For the battle paths
A terrible end to one
Whom is cut down to size,
The thirst for blood not gone
And the only prize
Carnage, carnage.

They roam the streets,
They are death-seekers
That feed on human flesh like sweets,
As they roam, the seekers
Walk, eyes peeled
For someone to rip the eyes
From the firm sockets, they squealed
In pain of the tearing feel of flesh ripping
Carnage, carnage.

Bones crunch, flesh squelches,
Teeth slash through skin
As one of them makes a belch,
No one human could win.
The evil-filled mutations
Were full of blood inside,
Of other unfortunate human nations
Came the pools of putrid rotten flesh
Carnage, carnage.

Death, guts, blood, rotting flesh
A main course of human
For an angel of death.

Ed Speller (13)
Meole Brace School, Shrewsbury

The Curse Of The Minotaur

Breath nearly ice,
Heart pounding rapidly,
Determined, petrified,
Sword ready to attack,
Shield ready to defend.

Pitch-black ahead,
I start walking,
The stench of blood,
Skeletons crowded with rats,
My only lifeline rolling away.

I had no option
But to follow the string.
My sword scraping the wall,
My shield in front of me.
I suddenly stopped,
I looked up.

There it was
The Minotaur
With its bloodshot eyes,
There gleaming at me.

The Minotaur charged,
I dodged it.
I struck the Minotaur,
It hit the ground,
It was dead.

I dropped my sword,
I picked up the string,
Then I ran,
My feet echoing,
I got out.

Damon Jones
Meole Brace School, Shrewsbury

The Rescue

I scramble out of a broken building,
The dust so thick I can barely see,
I hear no cries of any people,
I run to my home to save my daughter,
In despair I scream her name,
But no words come from my mouth.

When I speak the dust hounds my dry throat,
But I can't stop now I am in dread,
I run to the mound of dirt and rubble,
I lift the broken glass and brick,
I do not care about the pain.

I see her arm lift and fall,
She is gone, her ten years of life
Drained in bits of broken brick,
My heart is split in half by the very glass
That she is buried in.

Rosie Corsentino (12)
Meole Brace School, Shrewsbury

Space

I couldn't find the ladder to the stars
But meanwhile the men from Mars
Put space travel into my blood,
Then before the flood, I flew to Venus,
Where I swear I thought they'd seen us.

We took away for the moon
And told everybody we'd be back soon,
We thought and thought
Until we caught all our deep desires,
Then light the nights with our vast fires.

Then they told me I'd already lost
Even though I paid the cost,
But I've got my safety net
And all I have to do is make a threat.

Jack Sanders (13)
Meole Brace School, Shrewsbury

A Week In A Teenager's Life

On Monday I get up, sun shining,
The shining sun was blinding.

On Tuesday on my way to college,
It teaches me a lot of knowledge.

On Wednesday going to the shop
To buy my mother a blue mop.

On Thursday I take my sister to school
Where she learns some important rules.

On Friday I have a lie in,
Then I throw all my rubbish in the bin.

On Saturday I go to town
Where I see a great big clown.

On Sunday my family comes round,
There was a lot of noisy sound.

Sara O'Callaghan (12)
Meole Brace School, Shrewsbury

The Dark Tent

'T was like you had been wandering for
H ours, searching, searching all night long. The
E vening was dark and gloomy; I had been walking for ages,
   finding nothing at all.

D arkness all around me, felt like I had been swallowed up into
   an eerie place,
A ir, cold as snow surrounded me. Then I saw a
R ather strange light ahead of me, from a tent shaped like a
K ind of cone. As I walked closer the light got brighter and brighter.

T he tent was upon me now. I
E ntered through the door.
N othing was inside except a torch in the middle, on a stool, and
T hen suddenly a . . .

Aron Davies (13)
Meole Brace School, Shrewsbury

The Night Dream

It was like you have been searching all night
And you forget what you're looking for,
Looking into a dark black empty space.
(Drifting into a night dream.)
What to dream about, *whhhhhh* . . .
A clown in a bright yellow juggling suit,
With big red shiny shoes,
Size 13 and the clown is losing his balance,
(Everybody laugh out loud, ha, ha!)
Blah, blah, blah, so on, so on.
Twisted!
What a random word!
Tick-tock, tick-tock!
Why do clocks make that noise?
Why can't it be ding-aling, ding-aling?
What to dream . . . whhhh . . . whhhh
I know!
Come out of this night dream
And I will search for the thing I was meant to be searching for,
But what was I meant to be searching for?

Sophie Bishop (13)
Meole Brace School, Shrewsbury

Dance

D ancing all through the night
A cting for every step
N ext to a blinding light
C almly gliding across the floor
E xtending the glamorous sight.

Megan Wood (13)
Meole Brace School, Shrewsbury

The War

It was like when you have been searching all night,
All the bombs are crashing everywhere.
Where are all the children?
Where are all the cars?
All of the people are screaming for help.

The sky is dark and brutal,
The colours are black and deep,
I can't find anyone anywhere now,
It scares me. It scares me.

Every building is destroyed,
We're all like circus folk,
They're laughing at us, teasing us,
It's all gone now,
The twisted people, the twisted clouds, the twisted sounds,
The world can never be the same.

Andy Dunn (13)
Meole Brace School, Shrewsbury

Passion

I have always had a passion for horses,
On which I have tackled a lot of courses.
I have been riding all my life,
It's all been really, very nice.

I wish to carry on with this sport
And show off all of what I've been taught.
There's not one part of horses and caring for them, which I dislike,
From mucking out to riding all about.

I would love to ride professionally
And travel with horses all around the country.
Becoming a show jumper is my dream,
No matter how impossible it all may seem.

One day, I'll make my dream come true
And fulfil, everything I have always wanted to do.

Lauren Owen (13)
Meole Brace School, Shrewsbury

Through The Night Into Your Heart

It was like when you had
been searching all night,
I met you but didn't know
who you were or where I was.
We were everything together,
like the deep purple sky
against the stars.
Everything was so perfect.

Being with you was like
riding a unicycle,
I didn't know when
I could fall or go wrong.
You were like an angel,
heavenly in every way
but I knew inside
you were a devil.

You couldn't have made
me feel happier.
We were twisted together,
never wanting to leave.
It was like when you had
been searching all night,
I didn't know who you were
or where I was.
Now I know,
I was in Heaven and you
were my angel.

Kyle Arrowsmith (14)
Meole Brace School, Shrewsbury

A Potion To Be A Famous Footballer

Crush the eyes of Frank Lampard,
Slice the brain of Steven Gerrard.

Chuck in clever Mourinho
With the shirt of Jermaine Defoe,
Cut up stupid Swede Sven,
Jab his eye out with a pen,
Rip out Ronaldinho's teeth,
Chop off his head upon the heath.

Crush the eyes of Frank Lampard,
Slice the brain of Steven Gerrard.

Boil the quick feet of Ronaldo,
Throw in Zidane's blended toe
With the Man United's Van der Sar,
Best keeper in the league by far.
Cut off the hands of Joey Hart,
Slice them up and rip them apart.

Crush the eyes of Frank Lampard,
Slice the brain of Steven Gerrard.

The leadership of John Terry,
Drink his blood, it tastes like sherry,
Push in knocked out Ashley Cole,
Knock him out with a great big pole,
Melt the toes of Jamie Tolley,
Poke his eye out with some holly.

David Howarth (13)
Meole Brace School, Shrewsbury

The Moon Misses You

I sit alone and bleed away the hurt
In the grime and the dirt
And the angels sing softly to me
And the tears trace a path to see
I cry for myself and the life I lead
For all the things I don't have and need.

My internal scream is deafening
The wall I put up is crumbling
The repeated pain you put me through
My dreams are broken, my heart is too
Memories like cyanide raging in my blood
I see you as you really are clear as mud.

The path is dark, lit only by contempt
Rage for love and life, my debt is spent
The day you turned your back and the tainted lies
The year you walked into my life, I despise
I miss you like the moon misses the sun
But I dry my tears, my life without you . . .
Has just begun.

Anna Davies (14)
Meole Brace School, Shrewsbury

Nightmares!

It was like when you have been searching all night,
Searching for the morning day,
Searching for the light.

Trying to wake up from black and fiery dreams,
Stuck in time, stuck in space,
Stuck in a circus it seems.

As black as dead,
And as dead as black!

Will Alexander (13)
Meole Brace School, Shrewsbury

Ode To A Banana

The sight of your great curvaceous figure
Lying in the palms of my humble hands,
A view like this fills me with great vigour
That cannot be found in any other land.
Your smooth yellow surface is fine to touch,
The way it reflects the light is divine,
Some people do not like your look, not much,
But I am proud to say you are mine.
The sweet sound of your skin slowly ripping
Is gripping me down to my inner core.
Now your wonderful sweet taste is slipping
Down my throat, my body craves for some more.
Yes, I would trade a thousand sultanas
To bite through a beautiful banana.

Andrew Kirby (15)
Meole Brace School, Shrewsbury

The Night

It was like when you have been searching all night
And nothing but the street lamps are glowing,
Silence, except for the odd chirping from a bird,
The houses which stand out during the day are now lifeless.

The crowds of people have now died away,
All that's left of the circus
Are the posters drooping from the walls,
Oh I hate the clowns!

My tears are like the Nile flowing forever,
Nothing's the same,
The world is twisted,
When will it end?

Paige Walford (13)
Meole Brace School, Shrewsbury

The Rainbow

Red is fire burning away,
It's still there day after day.

Yellow is the colour of a bright day,
Taking our skin colour away and away.

Pink is the colour of love,
It's sent all the way from up above.

Green is the colour of crispy leaves,
They come from big tall trees.

Orange is the colour of a choco bar,
Imagine it as a bright orange car.

Purple is the colour I like,
But it has to be a particular type.

Blue is the colour of a clear sky,
Don't look up or the sun will make you cry.

Tineka Frost (12)
Meole Brace School, Shrewsbury

Vacant Eyes

Let me undo the black ribbon
Which ties your heart,
Scratch away your fears,
Peel away the dark.

A burning desire
That bitter taste of lust,
Vacant eyes
Watching your forgotten soul.

Your bloodstained hands
A disfigured mess,
Silently weeping,
Silently swaying.

Poppy Olah (14)
Meole Brace School, Shrewsbury

Hunger

Fly on my mouth
Staining my lips,
No strength
To blow it away.

Alien eyes glare at me
As I ruin their perfection.

I hold out
Unrecognisable sticks,
My disfigured
Bones.

Look away from me,
Protect your children,
Just too ugly
To pity.

You - with your
Full thin bellies
And me
Bloated, empty, aching.

Ignore me long enough
And I might go away,
That's what I deserve,
Isn't it?

It's my fault I'm like this,
Nothing to do with you,
So why should you help me?
Don't bother.

I don't need much,
Needn't spare me your love - just some food,
Perhaps you'll think about it,
But don't expect me to be there tomorrow.

Lucie James (14)
Meole Brace School, Shrewsbury

To Be A Footballer

Boil Beckham's foot,
Burn Zidane till he's soot,
Grate Henry's right leg,
Simmer Gerrard and make him beg.

Rooney, Ronaldo, Henry,
The best in the world will be me.

Grill Ronaldo till he's toast,
Then I will have a good boast.
Fry Heinz until he's hot,
Then shove him in the great big pot.
Burn the great Ashley Cole,
Then throw him in the hole.

Rooney, Ronaldo, Henry,
The best in the world will be me.

Robinho's left leg,
Attached with a peg.
Terry's big strong head
Along with Johnathan Stead.

Rooney, Ronaldo, Henry,
The best in the world will be me.

Tom Bowen (13)
Meole Brace School, Shrewsbury

Random

It was like when you have been searching all night,
Dark, gloomy owl screaming,
Bushes rustling, trees whining,
Foxes lurking about,
Owls flying around.

Black as night,
Badgers scurrying around,
Wolves howling,
Rabbits hiding.

Elephants making noises,
Splashing about in the water,
Making noises through their trunks,
Deer prancing around,
Going to their babies.

Vines are twisted all up the trees,
Like a staircase
Going round and round and round,
Up and up and up,
Making you feel dizzy,
Your eyes following it up the tree,
Twisting and twisting, winding and winding,
Never-ending then
Stop!

Abbygale Lewis (13)
Meole Brace School, Shrewsbury

Twisted

It was like when you had been searching all night,
When you ate some chips off your shoulder in your fight:

You screamed - you cried,
You danced in your might.
Yellow, black, green and blue;
Body as bruised as bruised can be.

Like a child at the side of the road,
You were washed out - beaten - thrown away.
Yet you had no hunger - you did not want to leave.
Of course! You had yet to make your peace.

It was like when you lost your mum:
Brothers in turmoil; and the whisky on the table.
There was no way to turn, nowhere to go.
Sat in your corner, you thought about it all.

You twisted around,
To being your round:
It was pound after pound;
Before he hit the ground.

Robin Kearney (15)
Meole Brace School, Shrewsbury

Humpty Dumpty

Humpty Dumpty sitting on a brick wall,
Singing merrily to a lovely tune.
Also bouncing his favourite ball,
Suddenly it turns to moon.

Oops-a-daisy he has fallen off!
King's horses and men come to see what happened.
As the horses eat from a trough
The king's men go to the back of the wall.

They finally find some tape and glue,
As they try to find where the pieces go.
His yolk hardens and turns blue,
Then one man shouts, 'I've found his toe!'

Humpty Dumpty back sat on the wall,
King's horses and men start heading back to the castle.
While Humpty starts bouncing his ball again, but feels sad,
But King's men go mad as the horses make such a hassle!

He's on the floor all shattered
And totally battered.
It's a really hot day so he starts to fry,
But the steam he makes, wants to fly!

Alex Edwards (12)
Meole Brace School, Shrewsbury

The Rescue

I cry out thinking, *where is my child?*
I tread carefully and cautiously,
I must find him.
Is he dead?
Is he alive?

On my hands and knees,
Oh, I can't find him,
'But I must,' I cry out.
Then in the corner of my eye,
Something moves, I go over,
But it's just one of my son's toys.

I hit my head on the rock,
Just then I think it's all over,
I see something peering up at me,
I clear the rubble,
My God, I've found him, it's him,
My son, back in my reach.

Ben Williams (12)
Meole Brace School, Shrewsbury

Anger's Emotion

The mental trap of human anger,
Released as one,
Like a cat out of a bag,
Or a bird of prey starting the chase.

The anger of the circus clown as it drops
Its juggling flame,
As angry as a dog, as his bone
Has been prised from his teeth.

The anger explodes!
Danger all around,
Panic and the twisted life stops.

David Alexander (13)
Meole Brace School, Shrewsbury

Teenager's Week

On Monday it's very sunny,
But school is not that funny.

On Tuesday we have maths all day,
But I think we should get to play.

On Wednesday we're on second lunch,
But there is nothing nice to munch.

On Thursday we have French,
But I would rather sit on a bench.

On Friday we're on the last day,
Why couldn't it be the end of May?

On Saturday I have football,
The other players are very tall.

On Sunday I like to rest,
But my sister is always a pest.

Charlotte Jones (12)
Meole Brace School, Shrewsbury

The Dream

It was like when you had been searching all night,
I just couldn't find my baby brother,
I must have been the most frightened person in the world.

My heart turned black when I heard him cry,
I wanted to shout Mum but my voice stopped working.
My brain was like a trapeze artist falling with no safety net, flying
                                                        like a brick.

But when I heard footsteps, I woke with a jump,
I saw shadows in the distance,
I was talking to myself, 'Is this some twisted joke?'

Lowell John (12)
Meole Brace School, Shrewsbury

Pied Piper Ballad

In the little town of Hamelin,
Rats were everywhere,
No laughter, joy or happiness,
The people were in despair.

They should have paid the Pied Piper,
Instead they turned him away,
If only they'd have known
The price they'd have to pay.

Then came the Pied Piper,
Who said he'd rid the town of rats,
He charmed them to the river
And that was the end of Hamelin's rats.

They should have paid the Pied Piper,
Instead they turned him away,
If only they'd have known
The price they'd have to pay.

He went to the mayor for his money,
But the mayor would not pay,
He was thinking only of himself
And ordered the Pied Piper away.

They should have paid the Pied Piper,
Instead they turned him away,
If only they'd have known
The price they'd have to pay.

The Pied Piper played another tune
And all of Hamelin's children ceased to play,
They ran to him from all directions
And he stole them all away.

Toby Pierce (12)
Meole Brace School, Shrewsbury

Elizabeth Green And The Sewing Machine

Elizabeth Green,
Elizabeth Green
Sewed her hand to a sewing machine.

Sewing machine,
Sewing machine
Stitch, stitch up her hand.

Her hand,
Her hand,
Her poor, poor hand, silly Elizabeth Green.

Elizabeth Green,
Elizabeth Green
Silly little girl that you have ever seen.

Ever seen,
Ever seen,
This little girl is a really silly fool.

Silly fool,
Silly fool,
'Elizabeth Green, how did you manage that?'

'Manage that,
Manage that,
Easy sewing up my hand it got caught.'

Got caught in the sewing machine,
Painful pain but didn't die.

Didn't die,
Didn't die,
That was lucky but still didn't *die.*

Anna Pemblington (12)
Meole Brace School, Shrewsbury

First Day At Secondary School

It was like, when you have been searching all night,
I just hoped I wouldn't get a fright,
Or get into a very ugly fight.
It was my first day at secondary school,
I just felt like I was such a fool,
We have to wear a blue sweater which is cool!
I made a friend, her name, Jen,
She says she has a pet hen,
She also has a circus pen.

I made another friend called Fred,
His hair was like a rose, just as red.

It was a very fun day,
I did forget my dinner money but I didn't have to pay.
I couldn't stop laughing, going, *hey, hey, hey.*
My lunch pass was all twisted and bent,
Jen gave me a pen but just for Lent,
People said to me that Jen is a gent.
I go home from school just after three,
My bus money ticket was quite a fee,
I got to my front door and thought I'd lost my key!

Sophie Putterill (12)
Meole Brace School, Shrewsbury

Think

I sit in the part where I dwell,
Thinking about life I thought I knew so well.
Life is short, life is sweet,
We have no time to sit and think
Living dreams, living life
Nothing guaranteed
So make the best of this
Life we have
And live every day as if it's the last.

Rachael Hollingsworth (16)
Rutland College, Oakham

Reality

Scorched hands out in front
Blood on my side
Everything passes by and by
Vague images pass, voices float
Family by my side
Numb with pain
What have I done? What have I gained?
Well here I am, look at me
What is there really to see?
My body torn, my mind mangled
Restless thoughts spinning
I can't breathe, I start to panic
I take a breath, my mind goes blank
I don't feel a breath, I can't feel my heart beat
Well here I am, look at me now, what have I become?

Meryl Harland (17)
Rutland College, Oakham

The Cure

One kiss of her lips, I melt inside,
I feel immortal with her at my side.
Now it's all gone wrong, he's out on remand,
My jewel stolen from the palm of my hand.
Running down my cheek, a warm, salty tear,
My angel flies, I watch her disappear.
I tried everything to get her out of my head
As I sit and watch my wrists run red.
Then . . . the most comforting friend I've seen in years,
Those two shiny barrels shall deafen my ears.
I dig out the shells . . . as I might have some fun,
Wearing red gloves, my wrists strongly run.
My head starts to clear, a cure for this pain,
She's out of my head . . . along with my brain.

Sean Doyle (16)
Rutland College, Oakham

The Coast

There she stands before me,
As I gaze at her deeply,
The anticipation burns within,
The vast expanse of pure sin.

The dominant figure shapes my fate,
As I lie beside her, as her innocent bait,
I mount before her, waiting to ride,
Dipping in and out like the tide.

Hold on, she's picking up pace,
I need to bail out and splash on her face,
My mast starts to strain,
I fear I can't maintain.

The seamen are propelled to shore,
To seek shelter for evermore,
The storm has now ceased,
As I lock up my beast.

As I approach land,
A fellow rider offers a hand,
I reply, 'No thanks,' as I lay my sail under many a cloud,
The new Tushingham 9.4 metre sail has done me proud.

Thomas Jackson, Joe Harley (16) & George Shelbourn (17)
Rutland College, Oakham

Obstacles

An obstacle, something in one's way,
Something that disperses people's dreams, ambitions and hopes.
Something that is said we should get over, under
Or in any way possible around,
To acknowledge and compete its existence shows ambition and drive,
So simply to acknowledge it shows defeat and sadness.

I have an obstacle to face and have had many before,
No matter how hard or easy I shall never give in.
To give up is the sea crumbling the harbour wall, washing us out,
A prey catching a lion's family.

Who is this girl I see? The reflected image of imperfection in the mirror,
Staring at me, telling me to give up is to give up everything I have
                                                    ever preached,
To disable my beliefs and dreams is to disable the life I've dreamed
                                                    of living
And is the end of my honesty and innocence.

I must carry on, defeat and abolish the obstacle and my purity
And significance will be regained.
I'm determined, driven and can succeed.
It may hurt others and myself
But for the image in the mirror to be perfection
I can and shall succeed.

Kelly Pridmore (16)
Rutland College, Oakham

Love Conquers All

To know eternity in a single second
To fly and soar on borrowed wings
To dip and dive in seas unreckoned
To spin around those golden rings
To listen and hear every thought
To cherish every precious breath
To never question what has been wrought
To be two as one in life 'til death
To walk together every day
To entwine for always, souls as one
To share in every single way
To go hand in hand until you're gone
    That rarest thing, breaching every wall
    Forever and always, love conquers all.

Charlotte Reidy (17)
Rutland College, Oakham

Exit

I stand here, not quite alone.
I feel the breath of the gentleman behind me,
And smell the sweat of the woman beside me.
Rocking from side to side, I only hope . . .
To avoid falling on either.

The cold, clean freshness of the air,
Encases me from head to toe.
My skin prickles, hairs are on end
Blood is surging through my veins.
A new lease of life, a sense of energy.
My relief is blatant,
As a gasp bursts from my mouth.

The horror is over,
The freedom to breathe is mine again.
The container has been opened,
I have stepped off the train.

Alex Addison (17)
Rutland College, Oakham

The Lonely Violin

Lying in the window,
Broken and abused,
The violin was forgotten,
Abandoned and misused.

No longer was it cherished,
No home to call its own,
Its tangled strings were lifeless,
No performance to be shown.

Just then the doorbell tinkled,
At last a sign of hope,
A little girl came pointing,
Excited as she spoke.

And soon the violin sang,
Just like it once had done,
Its bow no longer frozen,
A new life had now begun.

Emily Wilce (16)
Rutland College, Oakham

Unconditional

I look at her, she looks at me
I suppose some things are meant to be.
Love is strange, beautiful and real,
But this one is true as you should feel.

No matter what, she's always there,
Filling the world with love and care.
When times are tough, feeling blue,
I know I can count on you.

This love is special, this love is rare
For the one who cares is always there.
From birth, through life, she's the one
For this unconditional love comes from your mum.

Kayleigh Dolby (16)
Rutland College, Oakham

This Room

Darkness, melanoid black
Invading the empty space
Only clocks break the silence
Tick-tock.

When I open my eyes, no colours enter
I'm not provocative
Thoughts orbit the walls
Around and around.

I'm going to fail
Imagination with no equanimity
Thoughts go into reality
No control.

My head is stopping me
Nothing escapes from its solid walls
No emotion, no words, no movement
Nothing.

I'm going to fail, this is the end.

Charlotte Mills (16)
Rutland College, Oakham

Dressed To Kill

Jittering with excitement I close my till
Thinking about the night that's soon to spill
Out into the morning - when I'm bound to be ill
Skipping to the bathroom, I'm dressed to kill.

I meet my mates with a high five and a hug
One of them is always dressed like a mug
Skyscraper heels and a leopard print dress
She really does look like a mess
But after a quick turnaround she's dressed to kill.

Squished round a table - starting to sing
Wailing like cats - no care for a thing
'Bring on the cocktails before the last ding!'
Then it's out onto the cobbles - still dressed to kill.

Off to the club - will we get in?
Regular guy on the door - we're in with a grin
Dancing all night - oh s**t there's a fight . . .
Cor, he's alright.

Yes! We're dressed to kill!

Rozie Burgoyne McPhee (18)
Rutland College, Oakham

No One

Sitting in this cell I think back to how things used to be,
You used to be my teammate,
Or that's the way it seemed.

You plotted against me and I never knew,
While I stole and I lied and why?
Because you asked me to.

I would have done anything for you,
For us
To be together, forever, was all I wanted to do.

But now I know the truth, yes I do,
And I don't want to see you anymore,
But I'm still fond of you.

I don't know what to do with myself,
I love and hate you all the same,
I put my head on your shoulder,
You made me take the blame.

I want you to feel like I do inside,
Feel like you've just died. That's what I want from you,
You seemed so innocent,
So pure,
But now you're no one,
Nothing,
No more.

Daniel Wateridge (16)
Rutland College, Oakham

Adoration

A world without love,
A world without elation . . .

Interpreted by you, me, it,
To give and to hold,
To share celebration.
Rose-tinted eyes
Lead to bonds broken,
Lies, deceit and manipulation.
 Shards of trust once whole
 Leave time and space for contemplation.

A world without hope
Means only to exist.
A life half lived
To touch with no sensation.
Emptiness invades,
Like a whirlpool advancing.
 To manifest
 As we wait in anticipation.

Indelible memories
Tattooed on my mind.
Cleanse your soul and imagination.
Battles commence
Against the perfect enemy,
 But without such courage
 Leaves only provocation.

Harriet Bell (16)
Rutland College, Oakham

So Long . . .

The peaceful look upon your face
At least I need not worry
Now a spirit in a better place.

You look as though you're sleeping
A calming smile upon your lips
But I am forever weeping.

Your memory lives on
Although you may be gone
It hurts so much to try and move on.

You look so perfect lying there
With a hair not out of place
I'll say a little prayer, especially for you.

My friend so trustworthy and kind
A person so immensely true
A rare, yet special find.

Now a twinkling star at night
Gleaming, shining in the sky
Just like an angel in flight.

I'll never forget
Or let you leave my mind
Tell you that I love you -
Just this one more time.

This is not the end
So for now I'll say so long
Until we meet again.

Sian Webb (16)
Rutland College, Oakham

Uninspired Poetry

(Or 'Rubbish Written Late At Night')

I'm sitting at my computer desk
Staring at the screen
Trying to think of what to write
My brain's not very keen . . .

. . . to cooperate
It's late
And I'm not sure what to say
It really has just not been an inspirational sort of day

I'm sitting here
It's bedtime
And I've still not made a plan
Of all the things there are to write about
Not one of them, I can

I'm racking through my mind
I've started twice again
Every time I think of something
It's . . . 'What was that again . . . ?'

So here I am still searching
I'm writing in-between
Looking for the right thing
To make me seem a gene . . .

. . . ius, to all the world
Or maybe just my class
I'm running out of time
So just think of something . . . fast!

I really can't be bothered
I have nothing great to say
So let's just forget about this stuff
And leave you to guess . . . OK?

Fuchsia Wilkins (17)
Rutland College, Oakham

Social Outcast

The world passes by,
Time flows without meaning
I stand alone
Cast out by the intellectuals.
Rejected by the nobility
Given death by the magistrates
Society has left me.

Laughter is no more
Darkness engulfs
No place of comfort
No place of warmth
A social outcast
A misfit tall.

My screams fall on Death's ears
Light withdraws
Now I stand alone
Life without meaning
Numb to the world.

Hannah Morrison (16)
Rutland College, Oakham

One Day I Found You

One day I found you
Deep down inside
Frightened and scared
With no need to hide.

Digging deep down
Through the soil of the soul
Unblocking passages
And opening doors.

Then,
Like a phoenix
You burst out with gold
Shining so brightly
Brilliant and bold.

You bask in the sun
Your prison's no more
You circle around me
You swoop and you soar.

Now I'm complete
And we're finally free
The world will accept us
This way we shall be.

James Statham (17)
Rutland College, Oakham

Dare!

Will they see me again? I am not sure
But I will remember them, that I will
In Heaven or upon the light blue shore
We shall never forget that big old mill

Will my friends know how much I was afraid?
It was a dare I know, but to kill him!
But if I didn't, friends would be betrayed
I went inside, all the lights were dim

He was in there reading a horror book
I took the blade and stabbed his heart and limb
I felt cold, vile, scared, I did not dare look
Standing there in the dark, terror within

The blade hovers before my eyes, I see
Now I'm still here, but who's that next to me?

Jaweria Iqbal (12)
Small Heath School & Sixth Form, Birmingham

Depressed

There was once a young man in a wooden boat,
He had lost all his wealth and property,
Now all he owned was a box and a coat,
And a rabbit that went hop-hoppity.

He went sailing with no destination,
Trying to find a place to start again,
From a distance, he saw a plantation,
And all of a sudden, he became sane.

He began to row faster and faster,
But then, all of a sudden, something jerked,
The big box tipped, oh what a disaster,
Then out the water came a shark who smirked.

Late that day, washed on shore were his remains,
A life full of sorrow, death filled with pains.

Hafsah Ali (12)
Small Heath School & Sixth Form, Birmingham

The Grim Man

There was an old man who was truly grim
He was very disheartened with his sins
He was aware that his brain was so dim
He wanted to keep secrets locked within

He says it's because of the ruby ring
They had stolen from Sarah's collection
Now his head is hurting and his eyes sting
He has no choice, there is no selection

He trudges down the twisty lane alone
No one listens to his heartbreaking tale
Hear him drunken through his repulsive groan
It is not creepy it just makes you pale

Oh people what this man did, do not do
What he experienced, try not to go through.

Rehana Hussain (12)
Small Heath School & Sixth Form, Birmingham

Our Promised Land

Bruises, bruises everywhere, they hurt . . . bad,
Shaken violently in my childhood bed,
A pair of frightened eyes that look so sad,
It was my mother, this is what she said,

'We have to go now before he will wake,'
She went to the lion's den quietly,
Surreptitiously she took half the stake,
She tried to move secretly, silently,

The animal awoke from his slumber,
My mother took me and stealthily fled,
Eyes murderous and deadly like thunder,
If he caught up with us we would be dead,

I clutched on tight to her bruised, broken hand,
We had broken free to the promised land.

Jasmin Begum (13)
Small Heath School & Sixth Form, Birmingham

The Storm

A lighthouse keeper I had always been,
Until all was lost that fateful day.
My great sorrows they could not have foreseen,
So great my debt I owed, I could not pay.

Alone I drifted across the grey sea,
On and on, not caring where I sailed.
Alas good fortune had abandoned me,
In this life I had so miserably failed.

As storm clouds gathered, it began to rain,
The tide tipped my boat with a mighty roar.
I fell deep down to the seabed in vain,
I hit the bottom and I was no more.

But death could not keep me away from home
Where my lost spirit to this day does roam.

Ayesha Kausar Hussain (12)
Small Heath School & Sixth Form, Birmingham

Alone

I stand alone not knowing what to do
I watch all my fond memories go by
The odious food of divorce I chew
My wife had left me for another guy

And then I feel my body going numb
As I feel a chill trickle down my spine
I wish I could crawl into a haven
I wonder about her, maybe she's fine

I think about what she has done to me
And I realise that I'm all alone
In this big world she has left me to be
A miserable lost man all on his own

My hopes are shattered, dreams they pass me by
None to live for, I bid the world goodbye . . .

Umeh Humaira Yousaf (12)
Small Heath School & Sixth Form, Birmingham

Tears From The Past

Upon the hills of Everlessentine
Stood a feeble old man watching the night sky
He honestly believed it was his time
He just wanted some answers, *why? Why? Why?*

Memories of his life enclosed his mind
As the nightly wind blew on his torn face
It was simple answers he had to find
And slowly he remembered the chase

It was a long time ago in his youth
When the man was a police officer
A burglar had just stolen loot
And committed a vicious murder

Here lies the body of young Frederick Wild
He was the grieving old man's only child.

Mohammed Nasir (13)
Small Heath School & Sixth Form, Birmingham

Farewell Mary

As death awaits fair maiden Mary Bell
Life is so full and the joy never ends
One morning I received a call, 'Farewell.'
'Rest in peace' a message we all send.

We roam in her memories as our goal
We set goals, a way of remembrance
Two vandals attacked the poor soul
Rot in jail as we end the hunts.

You have life; Mary will be in a hole
You should be lucky, for life is a gift,
If you die early, death will take its toll
Enjoy all your life, don't let it drift.

I'll meet you in Heaven, God bless your soul
Farewell, farewell, my good friend in a hole.

Aishah Ahmed (12)
Small Heath School & Sixth Form, Birmingham

The Coaster

Going higher and higher, more and more
Until the high top just before you drop
Use all your energy for what's in store
It feels like forever, it just won't stop

The speed of the coaster rattled my brain
The acceleration made my blood rush
The velocity will send you insane
The swiftness and the turns will make you blush

A relieved smile on your face when it's done
Look at the top peak, are you feeling scared?
Thinking back it was nothing, only fun
Your thoughts are wild by all your rides shared

It was a great time riding the coaster
Adrenaline rush when it got faster.

Akeem Forrest (13)
Small Heath School & Sixth Form, Birmingham

Lonely Man

A man was looking at the midnight sky
Thinking of the memories in his past
He closed his eyes and he started to cry
He had a wife and kid that didn't last

His wife hated him because he was really mad
She left him 'cause he had an affair
Jack, the kid, was troublesome like his dad
Affairs couldn't stop 'cause it was a dare

Ugly she was, she gave everyone a creep
She knows a lot so she's probably a geek
Everyone thought she was from Wolf Creek
Other thing is she's got tomato-red cheeks

He walked past as she was giving him beef
But he didn't know she liked the chief.

Yousuf Ali (12)
Small Heath School & Sixth Form, Birmingham

Abuse

Bruises all over, she sits on the bed.
For slitting her wrists, a blade she has kept
For getting up late, beatings to the head
She needs to escape from the tears she's wept.

Lying on the street, her head on rough stone.
A figure helps her up, keeping her warm.
He leads her away, towards his safe home.
She lives there happily, no beats, just norm.

A knock on the door, the old family,
They want her back, she receives beatings right there
The stranger demands that they set her free
He ends up on the floor, dragged by his hair

'I won't return,' defiantly she said
A blow to the head, on the floor she lies dead.

Iram Naaz Qureshi (12)
Small Heath School & Sixth Form, Birmingham

Why Suffer In Silence?

There I was standing alone in the playground
Along came the three big boys up to me
They said to me I shouldn't make a sound
They hit me hard and bruised me badly

I lay on the hard floor bruised and hurt
They searched my pockets and took my money
Then they walked away feeling curt
I got up and walked home, it was sunny

When I got home I cleaned the mess and blood
It was too bad I wanted it to stop
I cried so much the tears made a flood
My mom saw me, she took it to the top

I learnt, to bully, no one has the licence
I should never have suffered in silence.

Adnan Khalid (12)
Small Heath School & Sixth Form, Birmingham

My Mum Told Me Not To Talk To Strangers

My mum told me not to talk to strangers
But did I ever listen? No not me.
I didn't sit watching Power Rangers
I was out in the big world, yeah just me

But when I disobeyed that rule I cried
I didn't know that evil people lived.
I was pushed but all I could do was sigh
It hurt being shoved in the dark so I hid.

It was late, I heard gunshots in the dark
I was scared so I tried to get home safe.
Something bit me, 'Ow!' like a shark
Who could attack in this dark, I was safe.

My mum told me not to talk to strangers
And when I did I was in all kinds of dangers.

Misbah Ahmed (13)
Small Heath School & Sixth Form, Birmingham

Walking Away

I see lights at the end of this tunnel.
Where am I going? Why am I going?
It feels like I'm falling through a funnel.
It's like I'm in a boat, rowing, rowing.

Tell me, oh tell me, why do I feel bare?
Nobody knows what it's like to be me.
Why do I hear sounds when nothing is there?
How do I put this, I am not set free.

With all of my troubles shadowing me,
Everyone's pushing me out of their way.
I hate it, I rage in anger, truly.
When I take my revenge, then they will pay.

With no one else here, I feel lonely,
I can't forget this, a true memory.

Aseel Mahmood (12)
Small Heath School & Sixth Form, Birmingham

Lost Opportunities

Yes, it's true, we met many years ago,
I can't believe he can't remember me,
After I had turned him down and said no,
You see I was so young, free and pretty.

Now things are different, life has not been kind
In times of misery, I thought of him,
You see true love is hard to find,
I often dreamed of what things might have been.

I was tempted to go and say hello,
That's when she walked in all glammed up and bright,
No wonder he did not have his head low,
She probably won him without a fight.

It was certain that they were meant to be,
That's when he noticed and said hi to me.

Aisha Mohammed (12)
Small Heath School & Sixth Form, Birmingham

Changes

Three sisters hold the burden of their life,
With their normal role slowly drifting by,
The outside world is what they sacrifice,
Lonely in their house they silently cry.

The only thing they have is each other,
And especially their sisterly love,
Because years ago they lost their mother,
Who's peacefully now in Heaven above.

They found out they have a special power,
A gift of love and power to endure,
Although problems may fill every hour,
All problems they will face, handle and cure.

As time develops their powers will grow,
They will never be burdened under woe.

Hassan Hussain (13)
Small Heath School & Sixth Form, Birmingham

My Neighbours

The woman next door is really creepy,
Whenever I see her through the window,
She sits on the sofa looking deeply,
When she sees me she sneaks down very low.

The man next door is extremely weird,
He dresses up like a young Barbie doll,
He is ugly, and has a long beard,
He's like a freak show or an ugly troll.

The girl next door has lots of animals,
She lets them roam free outside my mansion,
She hopes to own some Syrian camels,
And a grizzly that has to be Russian.

They may not be the best bunch to live with
But my motto is to live and let live.

Wahida Begum (12)
Small Heath School & Sixth Form, Birmingham

My Birth

I was born 10th March, 1993
It was during a slightly cold spring night
My mum had two boys, one girl before me
The first thing my mum did was hold me tight

The first thing I did was cry really loud
I cried because I was exposed to light.
Mum and Dad said I made them really proud
From that day on they never had a fight.

That night they named me Zain-Al-Abedeen
My youngest uncle suggested the name.
My grandparents and sister weren't that keen
Everyone else said it would bring me fame.

I love my parents and they love me too
To show them love, whatever can I do?

Zain-Al-Abedeen Banares (12)
Small Heath School & Sixth Form, Birmingham

Bee

Flowers in the garden grew nice and tall
The bees came buzzing through the grass to see
And the smallest one was called Baby Paul
Baby Paul wanted to be a big bee

So he too could go in the nice flowers
He gazed at them longingly and just wished
That he was big and had supreme powers
But his big fat mother tutted and hissed

She told him to stop wishing and fly by
He went with his tail between his legs
Along came a queen bee, she brought antennae
'Help me great queen bee,' he pleaded and begged

She attached it onto little Paul's head
Sending him smiling to the lush flower bed.

Shaista Hussain (12)
Small Heath School & Sixth Form, Birmingham

Life As A Gangster

Yes, they may call us dealers on the street
But really we are ordinary guys
They think we are scruffs and say we're not neat,
It was peer pressure piling up high.

But really we are ordinary guys,
So there's no need to be frightened or scared,
It's just rumours and the kids made up lies
It's not our fault but the way we were reared.

They think we are dirty, we are not neat,
We do graffiti and smash the phone booth,
It's all the pressure that makes us go beat,
Soon we'll lose money, mind and our youth.

People say on the streets as we pass by,
That we should crawl into a hole and die.

Shamima Akhtar (12)
Small Heath School & Sixth Form, Birmingham

Born To Fight

Heroes from the darkness with strength in arms.
When they are born they are destined to fight.
Many warriors will fight with their bare palms
The warriors lose faith but there is light.

Three boys with their footballs, that's all they have.
Two girls with the talent of a gymnast.
That's all they get to save them from the grave.
The bomb is here, their eyes show them their past.

Time is scarce, one hour is all that remains.
There is one that rises over the rest.
The weather shows dangerous signs of rain.
It's time to get rid of the evil pests.

The bomb is turned off, let's all celebrate.
Hooray, hooray, let's all celebrate.

Ruqayyah Noor (12)
Small Heath School & Sixth Form, Birmingham

The Fight Arena

The roar of the crowd carried him to it
Its single purpose to hurry the fight
He stood straight with fists clenched ready to hit
He stood there ready, enemy in sight

He said he could win, now he was not sure
The rumble was now about to happen
He was hit straight away right in the jaw
It had always been a game, something fun

The fight was over before it began
He stood depressed with his defeat at hand
He had lost now without a single fan
He was no longer leader of his gang

Just another fool wandering the streets
He was out of it all, out of the heat.

Nasir Ali (13)
Small Heath School & Sixth Form, Birmingham

The Rugby World Cup
(Through Martin Johnson's eyes)

I think of the day we won the World Cup,
For days we trained for that big game,
I'd trained until exhausted,
Finally the big game came,
And to win I was determined.
The Aussies like a herd of elephants,
Stampeding down the field,
Ready like a bull to take us down,
At last the ball was passed to me,
I had the ball, there was a gap,
A gap in their defence,
I ran like a cheetah, as fast as I could,
The try line was in sight,
I was almost there,
Only five minutes remained, I was going to score,
I dived, I scored and the crowd went wild,
I'd felt exhilaration and despair,
Exhaustion and elation,
I held that cup above my head,
The main feeling was jubilation.

Andrew Barnes (11)
Southam College, Southam

The Test

The clock is ticking, ticking time away.
I smell fear and anticipation,
Straining knowledge and determination.
I hope never to return to today,
Almighty fear is flowing through my veins,
Trying hard to keep my concentration
All of my energy's dissipation,
The sweat is pouring as I rack my brains.
Finally, the hard work is now over,
The relief is pouring into our heads.
The day has turned from fighter to lover.
So tired, our limbs are feeling like lead.
Happy we have escaped the dragon's den,
But in three weeks it will happen again.

Leo Parkinson (11)
Southam College, Southam

An Ode To Autumn

The golden sun rises in the frosty morning air,
To proclaim its golden beauty atop its heavenly throne,
Gilding the leaves of the great oak tree,
Standing tall and alone.

A sea of rustling leaves lie discarded on the floor,
A superfluous flaunt of summer sun,
Unwanted in the harsh cold of winter,
Devoid of laughter, joy or fun.

So the trees stand bare,
Flailing their mighty limbs in protest at the bitter breeze,
But still the wind blows and blows,
To rustle branches and steal the leaves.

So as the setting sun sinks into its inevitable slumber,
Staining the land with its rays of burnished bronze,
The valiant songbird sings one last song of defiance,
Lest there be a merciless winter.

Andrew King (13)
Studley High School, Studley

The Bullies

The bullies approach and the victim cowers
The bullies push the victim into the bushes and into the flowers
The teachers stare but don't move at all
While he gets smacked hard into the wall.

As the boy I know so well was kicked around and fell
I stopped to help, then I heard a yelp
And his head was covered in blood.

He was rushed to hospital,
He could die, that was possible,
But rest in peace my dear good friend up in the sky
You mend and fly because I know we will meet again.

The bullies at school were not expelled
But put on a school report
As my friend was dying they were lying
In laughter on the floor.

The group called 'the bullies'
Have picked a new victim
And again one of my very good friends.

The bullies will push and shove around
And kick people to the ground.
They will have no guilt or memories
But the thought of him dying will stay with me forever.

Anna Padfield (13)
Studley High School, Studley

My Pet Dog Missy

Happy and mad she loves to be
When I am sad she is there for me
When we walk she carries her lead
When she runs she has a lot of speed
Her coat is soft, her muzzle too
If she could speak she would say,
I love you.

Maddy Howells (11)
Studley High School, Studley

The Roller Coaster

Butterflies jumping in my stomach,
Fastened tightly in the seat,
My heart starts to beat,
Faster and faster.

Knowing what's coming up,
Seeing the big dip in front,
I'm not ready for this stunt,
I cling on tight.

I can't feel my hands,
Slowly we reach the top,
We edge forwards and drop,
I've left my stomach behind.

The track twists and curves,
Everything's a blur,
I think I might hurl,
I start to scream.

We're not far from the loop,
The g-force presses on my face,
This is a scary case,
We start to pick up speed.

I see the ground below,
I feel like I'm flying,
The ride is dying,
As we slow down.

We've come to a halt,
I feel my stomach coming back,
I need to find Jack,
So I can tell him about the roller coaster.

Jennifer Priestley (13)
Studley High School, Studley

Forever

Let me be your Churchill
Fighting from the start.

Let me be your Gandhi
Protesting for your heart.

Let me be your tinsel
Brightening up your day.

You will be my Jesus
To whom I shall pray.

Let me be your curtains
Shielding you from harm.

Let me be your bracelet
Your only lucky charm.

Let me be your toothbrush
Brightening up your smile.

Let me be your hairbrush
With you all the while.

You are my book
My only inspiration.

Let me be your deodorant
And stop your perspiration.

I will be a glue stick
Sticking us together.

Let me be your last amen
Forever and forever.

My love for you is like a prayer
It goes on forever,
Ever, ever, ever, ever, ever.

Don't be his . . .
Please be mine . . .

Benjamin Costello (14)
Studley High School, Studley

Little Mary

Little Mary was her name
Pressing buttons was her game.
She was small, pale and loud
And lived in a town named Trinckleproud.
Mary lived with her nanny
You see her mum, who was called Danny
She just could not keep Mary still
She then ended up taking a death pill.
Why? I hear you say.
Well here we go, it was a sunny day.
Mary had a magical dream
To buy a ton of ice cream
She had no way to pay for this
And her mum said, 'I'll give it a miss.'
She then started to steal all of her cash
And started to give her a good old bash.
Anyway. The little girl thought of pressing things.
She didn't care if it stinged.
One night she spotted something red.
So she slowly crept out of bed.
She went over to give it a press.
The button sank getting less and less.
Then all of a sudden there arose a poof.
Mary had flown through the roof.
You see the button she pressed was linked to a spring pad.
Little Mary really shouldn't have been that bad.
She was sadly now crumbled in the road.
In a messy little load.
Mary had disappeared. *Gone*
She had fallen for her nan's con.

Ellie Springer (12)
Studley High School, Studley

You're The One I Want

My feelings for you are so strong,
You made me right when I was wrong,
All those times I couldn't see
You were the one, who guided me,

You made my life a daydream,
You helped me cross the stream,
To all those days of happiness,
That I couldn't see.

You gave me sight so I could see,
You were the one made for me,
We were perfect in every way
Until it happened, yeah that day,

The day that you left, made my life hell,
Deep down inside my heart, you knew I wasn't well,
When I was weak you made me strong,
Now you're not here, will I be wrong?

Now you've made us part,
All you've done is broken my heart,
You made my life a misery,
How can you make it right?
Come back to me and fix my life.

Will my dreams come true?
Yes I wanna be with you
My heart thinks deep, my brain thinks strong,
You're the one I want, or am I wrong?

My life was great and was fun,
It was all because of you
You brought joy to my life,
You made my dream come true,
Now you've left, I'll be thinking of you.

Naomi Layton (13)
Studley High School, Studley

A Friend Like Mine

A friend like mine is what all people need,
A friend on time to catch you when you bleed,
She's the kind of girl that gets in a mess,
But who am I to say I think of her any less?
She is funny and sensitive, always there,
For she is a girl to treat you with care,
To see her smile as it lights the sky,
That in her I know will never die,
If I were her would I be great too?
For what I see in her, I'd love to do,
I couldn't put anyone in her place,
For I know what I'll have to face,
She is not gone, she will always remain here,
For I do not want it to show my darkest fear,
Beth, my friend, I will always be with,
I know from the sky she will always give,
What am I without a friend in my heart?
For nothing in the world could pull us apart.

Tasmin Jones (13)
Studley High School, Studley

Oliver

I've known Oliver since I was four,
I'm being his friend more and more,
He gave me a video to lend,
Him and me are such good friends.
He gave me a football book,
I was in so much luck.

He isn't a fool, he is cool,
I'm glad he is in my school,
I don't live that far away,
I can call for him every day.

Mustafa Razzak (11)
Studley High School, Studley

The Woman

Her long luscious hair -
The jet-black of the sky it looks up to.
Her deep blue eyes -
The tranquil blue of Mediterranean waters
They send an instant cool into you.
Her fingers -
As delicate as a fragile snowflake that melts on them.
Her slender figure
As majestically flowing as the violin that rests upon it.
Her mind and thoughts -
As complex as a spider's web.
And finally her words -
Soft on the ear and gentle on the soul
As it passes into you echoing all around
Filling you with ease and at the same time apprehension
You don't hear her words
You feel her words.

Richard Hyett (13)
Studley High School, Studley

The Bird Watcher

What's that looming in the fog?
It's the bird watcher silently waiting
For any bird flying or racing.
Sketch book and notepad in hand.

There's a sparrow, a kestrel too
A swallow flying while cows moo!
The ducklings and ducks are busy munching bread
And there's a pigeon shot dead.

The fox stalks it carefully
The bird watcher shoos it off.
His throat is itchy, *cough, cough, cough*.
A flock of geese fly away
In every direction night or day.

Kate Dodds (11)
Studley High School, Studley

Thinkin' Of You

The thought of you remains
Although I close my eyes
How did I become
So caught up in your lies?

You swore you'd never leave me
Yet here we are again
The same old smoke and mirrors
Why'd you cause me so much pain?

I need now to move on
That is what I should do
It's harder than it seems
'Cause I keep thinkin' of you.

Each new day brings a lonely night
As you're not here with me
I need to kill these demons
I want to be set free.

I will be moving on
You've found someone new
But it's harder than it seems
'Cause I really did love you.

Becky Innes (13)
Studley High School, Studley

The 9/11 Disaster

In New York City
Everything was calm . . .
There was the phone,
Then the alarm!

The rumbling of the thunder in the skies,
The low plane came screaming by.
Windows folded into star lights
As the onlookers tucked into their pies.

Now it had crashed and burned,
Air America lives no more.
Flames danced across the office floor,
No escape through the flying hatched door.

People crying in the stilled air
There was my brother lying amongst the rocks.
In the distance I heard some sirens,
It's as if they'd stopped the clocks.

Gemma Simmons (13)
Studley High School, Studley

No One Cares

No one cares if you live or die
Everyone says your life is a lie.

No one really cares

Everyone bullies you all the time
Through the rain or shine.

No one really cares

Your life is a waste, no use, no way.

But trust me one day they'll all soon pay.

Mandy Spires (13)
Studley High School, Studley

Comeuppance

You sit here now, all cracked and grey,
And you wonder what went wrong.
Your selfish past is catching up,
Your lies are coming back.
You stole from your friends and countless others,
Now you're paying the price.
You bullied beyond belief,
You're getting just what you gave.
How many people did you stab in the back?
How many did you ignore?
How many people have cried because of you
And how many did you abuse?
You sit here now, all cracked and grey,
And you wonder what went wrong.
Your selfish past has caught up,
And your lies are already here.
Everyone ignores you but you haven't been forgotten,
Everyone remembers you but nobody cares.

Ruth Foster (13)
Studley High School, Studley

Poppies

As they sway in the wind
People remember
The day the brave men died
On the 11th of November
People remember
The day they helped us in need

We wear a poppy
To remember
The day the brave men died
A two minute silence
To remember
The day they helped us in need.

Rebecca Hoy (14)
The National School CE Technology College, Hucknall

These Trenches

I sit here in these filthy trenches,
Longing for my family.
I sit here with my aching heart,
While some people sit here happily.

I think about going over the top
And surrendering my life.
I pick up my military gun,
And then sit down in strife.

I remember way back home,
When we walked to the pier.
We had candyfloss and went on rides
And I thought they were something to fear.

That night was something to remember,
I will never forget it for as long as I live,
But that may not be for much longer,
For my life I am going to give.

I climb up these trench walls,
And cry for the mercy of my Lord.
My hands are shaking, my life at risk,
But for my country my life I can afford.

Katherine Asbury (12)
The National School CE Technology College, Hucknall

World War

In the time of the world war,
Young men were battled, injured and sore,
As they risked their painful body,
Just for Britain their home country.

Tears were cried, blood was bled,
All over the battlefield bodies were spread,
All over those fields poppies grow,
To create the day me and you know.

Reece Sanders (13)
The National School CE Technology College, Hucknall

Poppy Poem

Poppy, poppy, beautiful poppy,
Makes us all remember all those people
Who died during the world war
Poppies are beautiful just like
All those people who died for us.

You see people crying, crying everywhere,
When you know it's happened to you
It makes you want to swear,
Swear on your life
You would never let it happen
To your son.

When you go and get your poppy
Remember that every little
Bit of money or thought counts,
But remember to go and get your poppy
And think about all the people
That died for *you!*

Shan Thompson (13)
The National School CE Technology College, Hucknall

The Day My Dad Went To War!

The cold night of 1914, Britain and Germany went to war!
It was a sad day for all,
families splitting up,
my dad had to go to war.
I was very angry and upset
my dad was in the war!
The day of the war happened
my dad was in the war!
A massive nine fives landed in our neighbourhood
my dad was in the war!
People dying!
my dad was in the war!
I saw people dying and in pain.
My dad is dead!

Lawrence Anthony Turton (13)
The National School CE Technology College, Hucknall

Lost

You fall so far down,
You feel as if you're lost,
Running towards the nearest light,
Not knowing where it could lead you,
Maybe into darkness, maybe into light,
Might lead you into happiness or sadness,
Might leave you bleeding inside,
Might leave you shining outside in,
Could leave you smiling,
Could leave you angry, upset or crying,
Maybe could leave you showing the smile off,
Maybe you could be wiping the tears off your face,
People telling you, 'Life goes on, it's not the end of the world',
Or people saying, 'Show your great smile off',
'I like you all happy' or 'I hate you like this, can't you be happy'?
Everyone knows how you feel,
But they don't, they think they do, but they don't,
Not many people understand, only those who have had this happen
                                                        to them.

Sarah Falconer (15)
The National School CE Technology College, Hucknall

Exam Tension

Walking to my exam,
Got to remember it's jam not ham,
Get all the questions right,
Mum said I might get a delight,
30 marks set for all,
Tension throughout the hall,
The teacher said one hour to go
And the paper in front of me I wanted to throw,
Never felt like this before,
But now I'm finally out that door!

Kayleigh Abbott (15)
The National School CE Technology College, Hucknall

The Thick Of War

The sky was a mournful grey,
As the troops entered the bay,
The area was deadly silent,
This war was going to be bloody violent,
A gunshot ricocheted around,
The men's heads did pound,
With the thought of never hearing another sound,
The war had begun,
The loud burst of a gun,
The beautiful sands became a deathbed for some,
The ME-109 was sure to come,
Then a shell hits the sands,

The sky was a mournful grey,
But nothing was near the bay,
The sands had become a graveyard,
Covered in bomb shard,
Guns lay still,
On the utterly demolished hill,
The ME-109 *did* come
And crushed the hopes of some.

Chris Hibbard (12)
The National School CE Technology College, Hucknall

Remembrance Day

Poppies are red, just like that blood that was
On the battlefields after the war,
To save us the soldiers fought more and more.
Blood, sweat and tears,
All the soldiers were full of fears.

We all wear poppies in remembrance of those brave men,
Who suffered in the war and to hide from the Germans
They made strong dens.
The soldiers were brave, they hid all their fright
To keep us safe, all through the night.

Jordan White (12)
The National School CE Technology College, Hucknall

Football

Football is crazy
Football is mad
Football's the greatest
It's a good laugh

Kicking with
My feet
Heading with
My noggin

Scoring goals
It's just buzzing
Serious on the pitch
Messing when I'm off

I've had some
Fun talking to you
And now I'm going home too!

Jasmin Bear (11)
The National School CE Technology College, Hucknall

What Does It Mean?

A room so dark, so cold
A table complete with plates
Knives and forks
What does it mean?

A leaf falling from a plane
In the midnight sky
What does it mean?

A forest of fire
Then darkness
And suddenly nothing
But the beat of my heart racing.

Thomas Sellars (11)
The National School CE Technology College, Hucknall

War

He was upset to leave her alone
But he wanted to fight
And to battle alone
He was a proud man and would fight to the end
He would fight for his country
And save his friend.

The lady she cried, as he said goodbye
With his helmet, his gloves and his mask.
He was going away for a long, long time
And she could only wait and pass the time.
He kissed her goodbye and turned his back
Never to see her until he came back.

The little child looked up at his daddy
With his big suit, he thought it was funny.
With a little wave and a kiss goodbye,
The child was not afraid
After all, his daddy would be back,
To play with him and to kiss him goodnight.

So as they parted one by one
The man left to the setting sun
To guns and bombs and to blood and gore,
Never to return to the family he adores.
So the boy grew up with a hole in his heart
And the mother mourned every day for evermore.

Sarah Dunstan (12)
The National School CE Technology College, Hucknall

The Haunted House

The door creaking in the wind,
Spiders weaving silver webs.
The black cat eating out of the bins,
Rotten fish and splattered eggs.

Into the spooky living room,
You see a sofa full of dust.
You will soon meet your doom,
If you eat the plate of nuts.

While entering the dark kitchen,
You spot red liquid dripping out the taps.
The broken cabinet looks ancient
And now you feel like having a nap.

Going up the stairs, into the darkness,
You step into the bedroom.
The bed looks like a rusty desk,
It doesn't look so safe, you assume!

You run into the gloomy bathroom,
There are bugs living in the carpet.
You quickly decide that soon,
You best get out the house and hop it!

You suddenly see a monster,
He starts to howl and scream,
You've woken up, it's morning.
Thank goodness it was all a dream!

Chelsea Davis (12)
The National School CE Technology College, Hucknall

Fear Of No Love

Fear of no love
Fear of not getting married
Fear of being left at the altar
Fear of getting divorced
Fear of seeing family dying
Fear of seeing family steal
Fear of not waking up in the morning
Fear of waking up and you're not there
Fear that this day will never end
Fear of my heart being broken
Fear of never fearing
Fear of running out of love
Fear of my children dying before I
Fear of days gone wrong
Fear that my love for you will end
Fear of not hating
Fear of laying awake all night
Fear of no love.

Anna Johnson (13)
The National School CE Technology College, Hucknall

Hungry

Glowing eyes,
Stomping feet.
Looking for something to eat,
Crawling round on the floor
Knocking from door to door.
Give me food! Anything
If even the size of a diamond ring.
I am so sorry to be rude
But could you please just
Give me food.

Ashley Vere (12)
The National School CE Technology College, Hucknall

My Spring Poem

The blossom starts to bloom
April showers fall,
Bees on pretty flowers
Berries on trees so tall.

Chicks hatch out of eggs
Bunny rabbits are born,
Frogspawn roams the pond
Whilst hedgehogs roam the lawn.

Every spring's so beautiful
Every flower around,
Makes me feel so happy
Even when I'm down.

So why do you spoil spring
With your factories and cars?
Just enjoy the season
How real spring seasons are.

Gemma Wayte (11)
The National School CE Technology College, Hucknall

Remembrance Day

Poppies, poppies, we know what they're for,
The soldiers who fought for us more and more.
The blood they shed, the tears they wept,
All those nights that were left unslept.
The homesick days and the guns that were shot,
The hours they spent thinking up a good plot.
Paper they used writing to loved ones,
The funny hours went by singing made up songs!
And these were the soldiers, who fought more and more
And that is what poppies are really for.

Sally Danby (13)
The National School CE Technology College, Hucknall

Alone

Are you another one of those people all alone, crying in the corner
you moan and groan?
Nobody to listen, nobody to care, nobody who knows you anywhere.
Walking down the corridors a terrible sight, until you get outside a ray
of light.
But not for me, oh no it's glum, handling my mom's messy divorce
and boyfriend (scum).
Nobody who loves me, nobody who cares, nobody who notices
me anywhere!
Walk back home after a miserable day, off to dear Mommy probably
been crying away.
Baby sister crying for milk she needs, I sure wish Mom could find
a nanny to lead.
But I am still alone, home and school, you would think somebody
would notice unless they were fools.
Alone with no one to lie in their arms, for comfort and assurance
that I wouldn't get harmed.
Nobody who loved me, no one who cared, I wish somebody would
notice me, just somebody somewhere.

Arlene Ndiweni (12)
The National School CE Technology College, Hucknall

Tears Of Sorrow

They brought Jesus to his knees, yet he held his head up high.
He said that he loved us, and it was time for him to die.
They had no mercy on him, as they nailed him to the cross.
I want us all to think of this, but not as if we've lost.
For how many of us, would allow our child to moan?
For God, our Father loves us, this He has already shown.
So wipe those *tears* of sorrow, and know that God's your friend
And He will be there for you, when the Earth comes to its end.

Kayleigh Henson (12)
The National School CE Technology College, Hucknall

The Dying

The roar of a gun
A scream of hell
'The tongues of dying men enforce attention like deep harmony'
As Shakespeare said.
I peer across the battlefield, a site of pure evil
Germans advancing two by two
With their bayonets twirling
Their guns whirling
And firing their lead bullets of fire
I take aim with my weapon of death
As all of my garrison do
Then a volley, a sound of fear
As 50 Germans go down in death
The pain, unimaginable
The other Germans fall down in despair, their comrades and friends
Their brothers, in arms
All dead.

My garrison advance all happy with victory, we think
We are half the way across when bullets whizz overhead
My men scream and run for cover
As projectiles of lead and worse
Rip through the flesh of men like beer through the mouths of alcoholics
We run to our trench, all covered in mud
Into the belly of our discontent
The belly of the beast as they say
The dying.

It is now very peaceful in the dead of night
Forever waiting for our doom
By gas or bombs or ways unheard of
Our doom approaches and we're ready.

Christopher Hunt (12)
The National School CE Technology College, Hucknall

Family

Your family are the people
The ones who really care
Your family are the people
That when you need them
They are there.

Your family are the people
Who love you no matter what
Your family are the people
Which are not to be forgot.

Your family are the people
No matter how bad they are
Your family are the people
Without them in your life
You wouldn't get very far.

Jaide Croll (12)
The National School CE Technology College, Hucknall

I Met A Butterfly

I met a butterfly today
Sitting upon a tree.
When I said, 'Good morning,'
It said nothing back to me.
I asked what it was doing,
But it refused to tell.
I asked if it was tired
Or wasn't feeling well.
And then it opened up its wings,
As though to wave goodbye
And flew and fluttered all around,
Just like a butterfly.

Lauren Sketchley (12)
The National School CE Technology College, Hucknall

The Peaceful Lake

All is peaceful,
The lake is still,
Pond skaters skim the surface,
Nothing to disturb the peace,
The sun slowly rises over the glowing horizon,
Illuminating the peaceful lake,
Thousands of colours are thrown across the smooth surface,
Hundreds of hues and tones at once,
It's quiet on the peaceful lake.

The birds burst into song
And sing their morning song,
But the lake is still peaceful,
The lake is like glass,
Smooth and clear,
It is peaceful on the lake.

Splash,
The lake is peaceful no more,
The rock shatters the glass lake,
It shatters and thousands of ripples spread,
Out further and further towards the shore,
The lake is peaceful no more,
Children shout jumping in,
Splashing, sloshing, swishing,
Through the clear, cool lake,
The lake is peaceful no more.

Once the sun has gone down the lake settles again,
The ripples settle,
Once again the lake is smooth as glass,
Once again the lake is quiet,
Once again the lake is still,
Once again the lake is peaceful.

Dominic Johnson (13)
The National School CE Technology College, Hucknall

Nothing

Nothing is nothing
That's all I can say
It lumbers around like
A boring school day.

It twirls and it spins
But can never be seen
At night it might
Fill your bad dream.

It can be black as black
Or white as white
And crawls around
The house at night.

It could be big as time
Or small as a flea,
It can be owned by you,
It can be owned by me.

But nothing is nothing
That's all I can say
It can be black as night
Or bright as day.

Holly Jemmett-Allen (11)
The National School CE Technology College, Hucknall

Under The Sea

Dangerous most mysterious,
Sharky but smarty,
Deep but asleep,
The creatures await in the darkness,
My very own fear of the sea.

Beneath the mists,
Becomes a list,
Of encounters that lie ahead,
But teeth lie on my head.

George Bentley (11)
The National School CE Technology College, Hucknall

The Forest

The leaves cackle,
The twigs crackle,
The trees sway in the piercing winds,
The wolves' howls are all that sings,
The darkness binds,
All who find,
The forest in the night!

Whoever finds the forest,
In the night,
Will never see the shining light,
Or bright days where shadows lie,
And will always be bound 'til 'dayness' dies,
So *beware,* the forest doesn't care,
Who it imprisons in the night,
In the shadows, out of sight!

John Maiden (11)
The National School CE Technology College, Hucknall

Imagination

Imagine a world full of imagination
People flying through the air
Just waiting for a dare!
Dark woods with hungry bears
Chases in the Wild West,
Your teachers taken as hostages,
Put into volcanoes,
But in the end it's just you
Imagining it from your vegetables.
Sleep tight.
Hope you have good dreams.

Andrew Jowitt (11)
The National School CE Technology College, Hucknall

Diving To Your Death

Standing in the plane one day,
Looking into my doom.
My head is filled with thoughts of fear,
I could be jumping into my tomb.

I strap the parachute onto my back,
Ready to horribly die,
I stand by the door, from where we jump,
We are about to fly.

I'm rushing and spinning,
This is alright,
Perhaps I'll die on impact,
Of this awful flight.

I try to pull the cord,
It doesn't seem to be opening out!
Let's keep hoping for success,
I'm about to dive into a bout.

I hit the floor,
It hurts my feet,
I grab my gun,
The enemy I will defeat.

I rush forward into the fight,
I see the plane from which I did the jump,
Rush down in flames
And hit the floor with a bump.

The crew have bailed,
They have all fled,
But they have survived,
Unlike me, who's now dead.

Luke Tait (13)
The National School CE Technology College, Hucknall

War Is Not So Pretty

As we train for war
We do not have the best of facilities,
For breakfast, slop
For dinner, slop
For pudding, slop.
Our beds aren't too bad,
An inch of mattress,
On a hard and stony floor.
When we get to training,
At half-past five in the morning,
We run five miles for the warm-up.
We then pass through the obstacle course,
First barbed wire then,
A swim through a tight tunnel,
About three feet wide and one foot tall.
Finally we train with the murderous weapons.
We go around a course, where there are models which we shoot at.
On our backs we carry 80kg of gear.
The armour is not heavy, which is a relief,
A helmet and light clothing is what we wear,
It is good for training,
But when we get on the battlefield,
There's not much that's going stop,
That bullet heading for your heart.
This is our warm-up for war,
Not so pretty,
Is it?

This was the bomb to end all wars
Did it succeed?
No.

Harry Petcher (12)
The National School CE Technology College, Hucknall

My Imaginary Friend

Someone who will always listen to me,
Someone who doesn't care what I look like.
Someone who'll be there when I need them most,
My imaginary friend.

Someone who won't laugh at me when I do something wrong,
Someone who'll listen to me without a word,
Someone who'll play with me if nobody else will,
My imaginary friend.

Someone who won't hurt me,
Someone who won't let me down and make me wait for hours,
Someone who I can create to stand by me,

But some day I'll have to let it go 'cause I'm getting older now,
But hopefully in the future I'll be able to see my loyal friend again.

Nicola Burton (11)
The National School CE Technology College, Hucknall

The Terror Of The Bullies!

Bullies here and bullies there,
All around me they swarm.
Angry bees aroused from their nest,
When will I be left in peace?

I run and flee,
'Cry baby,' they call,
I trip, all is lost,
They pound and steal.

I run, a mouse pursued by the cats,
They trip me up.
Crack, my arm breaks,
They run, leaving me all alone!

Charlotte Wadsworth (12)
The National School CE Technology College, Hucknall

The Storm . . .

Light flashes across the sea -
The world became exposed:
The lightning struck
And with it took
The echoes of thunder . . .

The raging torrent, once gentle swell
Capsized the creaking ship,
Men overboard,
In sea once more:
Crying with anguish . . .

The storm had passed, the sea at rest
The sailors on the shore:
Once more on land
Covered in sand,
Then began to explore . . .

Gentle slopes and rocky cliffs:
The backdrop of their camp,
Driftwood and straw
Were hunted for
Then left to dry when damp . . .

Laborious hours they spent at work
Knotting strands of straw
When near done
The setting sun
Was gone for night once more . . .

The morning dew, as thick as fog
Stayed silent on the floor,
For when the cockerel cried
Before sunrise
The sailors were no more . . .

For they had left upon the wind
As soon as they saw fit
For the wood and straw
They cut and sawed
Was now a worthy ship . . .

Ffion Naylor-Roberts (12)
The National School CE Technology College, Hucknall

If Only I Could Touch His Cloak I Would Be Healed

To actually know you are alone to the will of these secrets that eat
me away,
(In this bleeding silence, where is the light?
I don't know how to keep my heart beating)
Where is this light that never goes out?
Where are you?

Such a sudden rain, to wash away the pain:
Lying; a false claim.
I want a new start in all this rain,
Beg to be clean.
Looks: so appealing,
More than I can afford, but within my grasp.
(But everything is killing me with invisible knives
as I lust for something better).

Someone take the rags that I call clothes.
Burn the old.
How can I be so blind to You?
I can walk straight out of the cycle,
Into Your arms (the lame can walk!)
And those who cannot talk will open their mouths and talk.
The blind can see! And me, is there hope for me?
You.
I am more than crippled, more than dying.
But not alone
But not alone.

Tim Maiden (16)
The National School CE Technology College, Hucknall

It's With Me Forever

I leave behind my children,
There is hope in their eyes.
But I still see their tears and hear their cries.
Christmas comes and Christmas goes,
I may have died, but no one knows.

We're under attack! The terror sinks deep.
My thumping heart takes a giant leap.
My friend falls behind, I hear him gasp
And then his gun falls from his grasp.
He grabs my arm, I watch him die,
A tear falls down as I say goodbye.

I know I'll die, I know I'll fall,
The stupid government think they know it all
They paint a perfect picture of fighting and war.
But really, in truth, the conditions are poor.
The trenches are flooded, the rations are gone.
We go over the top singing our war song.

To die for your country did not bring fame.
It only brought sorrow, tears and shame.
It was never fun, it was never kind,
You can't escape, it scars your mind.

It will be there always, that hole in my brain.
It's with me forever, that feeling of pain.
I'm back in my home, I can't be the host.
No one can see me, for I am a ghost.

Nicola Jenner (14)
The National School CE Technology College, Hucknall

Bonfire Night

B urning flames
O ngoing fun
N ice fun foods
F unky fireworks
I nspiring colours
R elighting the sky
E xtra toffee

N on-stop goodies
I nteresting sounds
G reat loud bangs
H appy faces
T winkling eyes.

Jessica Bestwick (11)
The National School CE Technology College, Hucknall

Poppy Day

I sit here in these filthy clothes
Longing for some friends
Some people sit and write to their loved ones
I just sit and cry
I want my family back . . . I want to go home
I try to sleep to stop the tears
I hide my face as the bombs come down
My helmet rattles
My gun shakes
My body freezes
My eyes close
I feel nothing . . .

Ashton Mayes (13)
The National School CE Technology College, Hucknall

The Playground

Happy faces fall out of the door,
A sense of excitement fills the air.
Break time has come, freedom is here,
Grinning faces everywhere.
Little kids gossiping like adults,
Whispering together and secret-sharing.
A sound of giggling and laughing,
Everyone seems so kind and caring.
The playground smiles at the adventurous kids,
Who run and play, whatever the weather.
A place of safety and security,
To watch is always a pleasure.
The past lesson has been forgotten,
The children all run together happily.
The entranced teacher just stands and watches,
The children all play so excitedly.

But in the corner he sits and hides,
As tears stream down his cheeks.
He is isolated, alone, unloved,
No one has spoken to him for weeks.
They push him, hit him, poke him
and then just laugh when he cries.
The playground is unsympathetic,
He curls up, hated and despised.

Nicola Maiden (14)
The National School CE Technology College, Hucknall

Autumn

Copper treasures draping the trees before they cascade to
the dewy ground.
The gentle breeze whirls them into the heavens and delicately brings
them back to earth.
Birds carol as they get ready for winter.
Children frolic in the leaves as the adults rake up the foliage.
But winter is here and autumn will be gone.

Sophie Platts (12)
The National School CE Technology College, Hucknall

A Table Tennis Poem

The score was 2-1, it was close,
The ball hit the post,
Everyone was ready to jump up and shout, hooray!
The coach said, 'Are you ready to play?'
The players jumped to and fro, are you ready to go, go, go?
Half an hour later the game was still in,
The other group was going down in the bin,
It was closer than two sharp pins,
The dancing cheer leaders especially the twins were ready to jump
Up and cheer the house down!

Danielle Abbott (11)
The National School CE Technology College, Hucknall

The Year

Spring has come at last
The flowers are now in bloom
And the small calves have just been born
And the sky has a blue moon
Yippee, spring is here!

Summer is here at last
People are drinking from cold cans
The sun in the sky is flying high
Thousands of people are getting tans
Hooray, summer is here!

Autumn has come at last
Bonfires burn in the black of the night
And colourful leaves litter the floor
The wind is blowing good enough for kites
Jump for joy, autumn is here!

Winter is here at last
The white snow is falling
And the Christmas trees are growing
The little robins are calling
Shout out loud, winter is here!

Amie Bottley (11)
The Summerhill School, Kingswinford

The Poetry Competition

There once was a girl with red hair,
Who tried to write a poem with care,
She sat up all night
And thought what to write,
But instead fell asleep in her chair.

She awoke with a fright
And began again to write,
She wrote on and on,
Till the morning had gone
And her room was filled with sunlight.

When the poem was done,
She sat in the sun
And looked at what she had written,
Then she filled in the form and pulled on her coat
And off to the postbox she did run.

Selena Malone (11)
The Summerhill School, Kingswinford

The Friendship Rose

You are my friend
And I hope you know that's true.
No matter what happens
I will stand by you.
I will be there for you
Whenever you need me,
So just call on me
When you need me,
My friend.
I will always be there
Until the end.
I am caring and loving
To you and to others.

I am so glad
You're my friend.

Rylie Jones (11)
The Summerhill School, Kingswinford

Skateboarding Poem

The churning of concrete is all I can hear,
As I ride up to the stairs with a dosage of fear,
Ten feet below, the pavement stares up
And I wonder whether I'm going to land this huge drop,
As I'm getting closer my heart begins racing
And I realise the size of the challenge I'm facing,
But mind over matter is all that I need,
As wheels leave the ground I hope I'll succeed,
One moment seems forever when you're up in the air,
After years of skating you learn not to care,
But when you're flying like that it's all making sense,
The landing coming closer, my legs start to tense,
But just for that rush it's all made worthwhile,
Shock running through my legs as I hit that hard tile,
Riding away with a grin on my face,
Away from my fears at an almighty pace.

Luke Breakwell (11)
The Summerhill School, Kingswinford

England Vs Poland

The crowd chants,
'England! England! England!'
The noise swims round the stadium,
The air is filled with excitement, apprehension, tension,
The players appear,
The noise grows louder, louder,
The ball is placed upon the spot,
First kick of the game,
'At half-time it is 1-1,' the commentator says,
The crowd goes wild waiting for the players,
The second half begins and England attack,
'Oh, oh, wonderful! What a goal by Frank Lampard,
England are 2-1 up.'
15 minutes left, England winning,
Poland attack and almost score,
But at full time it's 2-1 to England,
'And England are through to the World Cup!'

Scott Adam Wassell (12)
The Summerhill School, Kingswinford

Seasonal Flowers

Flowers in the spring
Are just opening out,
All different colours,
Yellows that shout.

Flowers in the summer
Are beautiful and bright,
All different colours
Pink, that's a wonderful sight.

Flowers in the autumn are dying,
Petals all over are flying.
Poor little petals.

Flowers in the winter
Are just beginning,
Buds all green,
Buds that are grinning.

Ellie Oldacre (11)
The Summerhill School, Kingswinford

Fizzy Drinks

They all go pop, they all go whizz.
They all go plop, they all go fizz.
I love them and they love me.
My favourite is lemonade.
I love to drink it in the shade.

When I drink it I close the door
And I drink it through a very big straw.
Oh fizzy drinks how I adore
Please give me, *more, more, more.*

Harry Beasley (12)
The Summerhill School, Kingswinford

There Once Was A Wacky Professor

There once was a wacky professor,
Who lived with a mad hairdresser.
They lived in a two-bedroomed flat
And kept a really fat cat.

Whilst reading The Mail on Sunday,
They decided to go on a holiday.
'Everything here is so dull,' they said,
'I'd like to go somewhere to clear my head.'

So off they went together
The professor and the hairdresser.
They saw a sign saying,
Get Away, Take A Piano Cruise Today.

They decided then that that was it,
They had to get on a really big ship,
Which would take them to places where the sun always shone,
Their bosses wouldn't notice they were gone.

So they went off to whole new places
And saw a load of strange new faces.
They went to islands warm and sunny
And spent lots and lots of money!

They went off to the Bahamas,
Where the hairdressers thought they kept llamas,
But no they kept something better instead,
Dancing monkeys with hats on their heads.

There once was a crazy professor,
Who lived with a Caribbean hairdresser.
While reading The Mail on Saturday,
They decided to go to a matinee . . .

Chloé Travers (11)
The Summerhill School, Kingswinford

My Best Friend Olly The Ferret

He runs all about, up and down,
Left and right, also down town.
They are amusing animals,
He gets wet when he jumps in the humungous swimming pool.

When he lies on my back,
He is as luxurious as a miniature blanket.
While they run around they don't make a sound,
As his feet tiptoe on the ground.

As he goes back into his home,
He curls into a big furry dome.
Then he falls asleep in a heap,
He looks like a cute little baby.

When he wakes up he's like a tiny bear,
As he yawns and wanders about.
When he eats all of his food,
He goes into a fun, happy mood.

As he plays through the day,
He loves to dance in May.
In the end he is just a ferret,
But he's my *best friend!*

Andrew Randle (11)
The Summerhill School, Kingswinford

The Evils Of Winter

Winter's weather is cold and harsh,
As it digs its sharp, jagged teeth into its prey.
The sun is trapped and can't break free,
We're prisoners in our own land.

It sends a blanket,
White and cold,
Which makes us shiver
As we try to get rid of this treacherous beast.

The tree's bony fingers reach out to catch us,
Rain crashes down
And the thunder roars like a tiger.
Gleaming silver sheets of ice cover our land.

The sun begins to attack,
The clouds are taken by surprise.
Snow starts melting
As the thunder backs down.

Spring has arrived,
New and fresh,
We have defeated this restless beast
And now can live in peace.

Sophie Ball (11)
The Summerhill School, Kingswinford

My Cats

My cat likes to play,
He'll do it all day,
But when he gets tired,
He likes to nap,
As he curls up on my lap.

My cat is small, pudgy and soft,
He likes to sleep up in the loft,
He is all round,
Doesn't make a sound
Because he's my fat little cat.

My cat likes to eat,
She always wants a treat,
She is very loud,
But as light as a cloud
And she always makes me proud.

My cat was soft, quiet and sweet,
But he didn't really like to eat,
He would sleep most of the day,
Didn't really want to play,
But I loved him anyway.

My cat was fast,
Went out all night,
But one day gave us a fright,
He wasn't very well one day
And very soon passed away.

Anna Stewart (11)
The Summerhill School, Kingswinford

My Opinions

In my opinion,
Family is important,
Because you only get one family.
In my opinion,
Friends are important,
Because good ones are hard to find.
In my opinion,
Knowledge is important,
Because it helps us live better.
In my opinion,
Health is important,
Because we only get one body.
In my opinion,
Fun is important,
Because it makes life good.
In my opinion,
Love is important,
Because we then have something to live for.
In my opinion,
Everyone is important,
Because everyone is equal,
In my opinion,
The people I don't like
And their opinions
Are still important.

Theo Barfoot (11)
The Summerhill School, Kingswinford

The Sounds At The Seaside

Crashing waves roaring at the cliffs,
These are the sounds at the seaside,
Donkeys' bells jingling along the beach,
These are the sounds at the seaside.

Children screaming with utter delight,
These are the sounds at the seaside,
Ice cream van's bells ring merrily,
These are the sounds at the seaside.

The song from the funfair on the pier,
These are the sounds at the seaside,
Seagulls screeching greedily,
These are the sounds at the seaside.

Spinning reels of the fishermen,
These are the sounds at the seaside,
Rustling papers from the fish and chip bars,
These are the sounds at the seaside.

The boats and ships soaring through the sea,
These are the sounds at the seaside,
Calm waves roll in peacefully as the sun sets,
These are the sounds at the seaside.

Jade Wilde (11)
The Summerhill School, Kingswinford

Fizzy Pop

A nutty professor sat pondering one day.
'A new type of pop, I must develop a way,
To invent a new tasty flavour of pop
For everyone to enjoy,' exclaimed Professor Flop.
'Once this is done,' he said very loud,
'It will be an achievement to make me feel proud!'

He sat deep in thought, confusion etched on his face,
What flavour of pop would people like to taste?
Cucumber, pumpkin, carrot or pea,
He hadn't a clue, why couldn't he see
That kids liked sweet things not vegetable flavour?
They liked sugary treats to enjoy and to savour.

Now Professor Flop was a nice enough chap
But his inventions were prone to the odd mishap.
The machine that was designed to give the pop its fizz
Began making noises like crash, bang and whizz!

After hearing the noise and upon all of the clatter,
Professor Flop crashed into his lab
To see what was the matter.

He realised his dream was over,
As he trudged toward the door
He turned and had one more glance,
At the broken pieces on the floor.

Beth Rogerson (11)
The Summerhill School, Kingswinford

Lemon And Lime

My name is Robin and this is my rhyme,
To some people this is a crime.
I really like a lemon and lime,
But some people prefer a dime.
A lemon and lime has a fizzy taste,
I never let a bit go to waste.
It is a bogey colour but I don't care,
Because I can get a lot at the fair.
If I'm too hot,
I'll want some pop,
That will be a lemon and lime.
I ask my mum, 'Can we go to the pub?
I want a lemon and lime.
Lemons are yellow, limes are green,
those are the juiciest fruits I've ever seen.'
My mum says, 'We are going to the pub.'
So I shout out, 'Hooray!'
As we are driving to the pub,
I say, 'I want a lemon and lime!'

Robin Rossmann (11)
The Summerhill School, Kingswinford

A Busy Day At The Seaside

Lost of people splashing in the sea,
Look underwater, what do you see?
There are pretty fish swimming around,
I scare them as I tread on the ground.
Look at the children with bucket and spade,
Lots of sandcastles children have made.
People everywhere collecting shells,
With each new find brings exciting yells.
Long queues waiting at the ice cream van,
With money ready they pay the man.
Punch and Judy gives us lots of fun,
Sitting down and laughing in the sun.
Sunbeds and umbrellas on the beach,
With sunburned men charging £5 each.
Seagulls screeching looking for my bread,
I hope they do not land on my head!
I catch a crab in my fishing net,
I hope I can keep it as my pet.
The tide comes in and the sun goes down,
I go home very happy and brown.

Charlotte Turner (11)
The Summerhill School, Kingswinford

Football Mad!

The whistle blows and the game kicks off,
The crowd starts to go wild,
It's Ronaldo on the ball,
He has a shot and it's a goal,
1-0 to Man U.

It's a kick off to Arsenal they've kicked off,
Neville goes in for a tackle,
He gets the ball and Perez goes in,
He slide tackles and cripples Gary Neville.

Perez gets a red card and goes off the pitch,
It's a penalty to Man U,
Ronaldo takes it and it's a goal,
Let's see the replay it's one heck of a goal!

The whistle blows half-time with Man U 2-0 up,
Two minutes into the second half,
Ronaldo has to change his boots,
His old boots have split.
Ronaldo's on the ball and approaches the goal mouth.

The linesman puts his flag up,
The offside rule's in play,
It's a free-kick to Arsenal and Thierry Henry takes the ball,
He passes a long ball to Ferdinand,
He strikes it into the goal, 2-1, a win!

Nick Page (11)
The Summerhill School, Kingswinford

Football

The whistle blew to start the match,
The crowds went wild.
The fans went crazy for their team,
Willing them to win.
Man U vs Chelsea.
Man U have the ball.
Terry tackles like a tiger and wins the ball.

Rooney takes a shot, the crowd goes wild,
The ball blasts into the back of the net.
1-0 to Man U, the reds go wild,
The whistle blows to start the match over again.
Chelsea have the ball.
Terry takes a shot, the ball whistles into the crowd,
And the crowd go wild for their team.

Van der Sar takes the goal kick,
Rooney holds it up and he takes a shot,
It just skims the post to go out for a goal kick.

Petr Cech hits it for Chelsea.
Ronaldo tackles like a lion,
Ronaldo kicks it up
And the whistle blows to finish the match,
Man U go crazy, the crowd go wild for their team.
Chelsea hadn't lost a match,
Now they have, Man U 1-0.

James Hill (11)
The Summerhill School, Kingswinford

Suicide

I used to take it for granted
You being there for me
Why couldn't I see
That it would never be.

Until that day you left me
Like a sailor lost at sea
You left me all alone
Now I'm on my own.

The sound of screams still haunt me
As I lie awake at night
Why did you pull that trigger
And throw away your life?

I still can see you now
As clear as the day
You pulled that bloody trigger
And drifted far away.

Your past and your future
You could only know
Your reason for leaving
I will never know.

Paige Korbel (13)
The Wakeman School, Shrewsbury

The Woods

The woods
They can be dark and scary . . .
Or light and cheerful
This one is haunted

There is a tale about the birds here
They do not sing - they are quiet and forlorn
The animals do not come out at night
Even the owls fly in sunlight
At night-time something happens

The leaves rustle and the logs crack
No light save an eerie glow of green
For every night something happens
Footsteps sound among the trees
The sounds of a cloak swishing

I once went into this most spooky of places
I hid in the treetops
And something passed below me
A dark object, like a person in a clock
Save it was not human

I made no sound, yet it looked upwards
And I saw its ghastly face
Wrinkled and grey
Shadows pouring over it
And it had a mouth of razors

I shall never forget that most ghastly of images.

James Pereira (12)
The Wakeman School, Shrewsbury

I Hate It When . . .

People follow me around.
People think that they're better than me.
You pretend you don't know me.
You don't talk to me.
You don't think of me.
You cry.
You don't smile at me.
You walk away from me.
We don't make up.
You make me sigh
When you turn me down.
You think of me as a friend.
You hate me.
We're not alone.
You're not there.
You put down the phone.
You don't call.
But most of all I hate it when we fight.

John France (14)
The Wakeman School, Shrewsbury

A Poem On Time

I went to London to see the clock tower
How many minutes in an hour?
60 I hear you say
But how many hours in a day?
24 I hear you say
Time is something we can't do without
We know this without a doubt
It reminds us when to eat
And reminds us when to sleep
Sometimes it goes slow
Sometimes it goes fast
But sooner or later it will all be in the past!

Ryan Flannery (12)
Thomas Telford School, Telford

Sun

I look out of the window,
Sun!
Another beautiful day,
A day to be outdoors.

I look out of the window,
Sun!
I like the sun,
I might go sailing today.

I look out of the window,
Sun!
I open the window
And smell BBQs cooking.

I look out of the window,
Sun!
I can see birds flying,
But can imagine the beach.

Mitchell Hill (12)
Thomas Telford School, Telford

The Kiss

My mother said, 'There were no joys
In ever kissing silly boys,
Just one small kiss or one small squeeze
Can land you with some foul disease.'

Last week when coming home from school
I clearly forgot Mum's golden rule.
I let Tom Young, that handsome louse
Steal one kiss from behind my house.

Oh, woe is me! I've paid the price!
I should have listened to advice.
My mum was right one hundredfold
I've caught Tom's horrid runny cold!

Chloe Simister (12)
Thomas Telford School, Telford

Time

I travel the world and outer space,
Wherever I go it's a different place.
There are strange people everywhere,
But when you walk past they stop, look and stare.
The planets all colours, red, blue and green,
There is always a different sight to be seen.
The way you travel is up to you,
By rocket, machine or a friend can come too.
You will explore the planet,
And have lots of fun,
But remember there's always work to be done.
Be amazed with all the information,
But try to resist the brilliant temptation.
You look down on Earth,
And think in your mind,
I am really enjoying this peaceful time.
But soon for me it will be time to go,
But the time won't go fast but very slow.
The Earth is so small from where I stand,
It almost looks like a circle of sand.
I am travelling down, I've had a wonderful time,
And I still have the memories close in my mind.

Kate Marshall (13)
Thomas Telford School, Telford

The Dark

I love the dark because
It is a home to fireworks.

The dark is . . .
As black as the inside of your body,
As black as the deepest, darkest oceans,
As black as the black at the end of the universe.

I love the dark because
You can hide in it.

Kirsty Harris (11)
Thomas Telford School, Telford

The Seasons' Genie

I'm bored of this cold winter
Now don't call me a whimper
I wish it were spring
'OK,' said a voice.
Now there are flowers
Wishes have wonderful powers
No snow.
But it is raining so I wish it was summer.
Bang! It is boiling hot
Sand on every spot
No rain
But I itch like mad with sunburn, I wish it were autumn.
Pop! A cold wind on my face
Red and yellow leaves falling at a steady pace
No it's not for me
I think I'll stay in winter
'OK,' said the voice.

Jack Leech (12)
Thomas Telford School, Telford

My Weekend

Friday when I come from school,
I go to piano which I think rules.
On a Friday big housework night,
And that gives me such a fright.

On a Saturday up at ten,
Go and clean out my rabbit's pen.
Then we go up town to shop,
Until my mum is ready to drop.

Sunday morning up quite late,
Have some bacon then wash my plate.
All day Sunday on my feet
Then I do my homework for the week.

Laura Roper (12)
Thomas Telford School, Telford

Magic Box

(Based on 'Magic Box' by Kit Wright)

I will put into the box . . .
the spark of a silver star on a summer's night,
tears from the eyes of an innocent phoenix,
the shadow of the milky moon in the sky.

I will put into the box . . .
the brightness of a shining emerald,
the darkness within the Minotaur's lair,
the rumble of the wild Atlantic.

I will put into the box . . .
the true story of my ancient uncle,
the whispered words of death from a dark angel,
the fatal cry of a leopard.

I will put into the box . . .
the drone of a demon vacuum cleaner,
the lost spirits of an unknown kingdom,
the intense flames of a Chinese dragon.

My box is fashioned with ice and silver and steel,
with a gold lid and whispers in the corners,
its hinges are the joints of a human.

I shall have adventures in my box,
through the maze and up to Mount Doom
with many battles to fight and many memories to keep,
and I will die in my box, with the sword of my own
and I will wash away on the Hawaiian beach.

Nathan Sanghera (12)
Thomas Telford School, Telford

Time - Haiku

Time is important
It takes us throughout our lives
Time can never stop.

Warren Beards (12)
Thomas Telford School, Telford

My Dog

My dog is called Milly
She can be rather silly
She sits at the door
To show when she's bored
But most of the time she is happy.

My dog is a Staffordshire bull terrier
And every day she gets even heavier
She eats lots of food
And is very crude
And then she is even happier.

And that is my dog called Milly
Who can be very silly
She eats lots of food
And is very crude
Till she is even happier.

Hayley Davies (12)
Thomas Telford School, Telford

Time

Time, time passing by,
Flying through the starlit sky,
Rushing, rushing all around,
Even rushing underground.

Ticking, ticking every day,
Ticking all your life away,
Tick-tock, tick-tock,
That's the noise that makes the clock.

Father Time, he once said,
'Use your time wisely or you may as well be dead,
Look around you every day,
And make the most of every day.'

Rebecca Percox (12)
Thomas Telford School, Telford

Autumn's Coming

Run little squirrel,
Run and have a rest,
The winter's coming fast now,
It's time you went to nest.

The summer has now ended,
The autumn's just begun,
The morning birds are singing,
All the children having fun.

Run little squirrel,
Run and have a rest,
The winter's coming fast now,
It's time you went to nest.

The leaves are turning crisp,
The trees are turning bare,
As they wisp round and round,
In the winter air.

Run little squirrel,
Run and have a rest,
The winter's coming fast now
It's time you went to nest.

Lara Vail (12)
Thomas Telford School, Telford

Football

F ootball is fantastic fun, playing for the Panthers.
O ff we go down the pitch.
'O h yeah,' we cheer as we score again.
T ackling hard we win the ball.
B ang! Tanis scores another goal.
A ll the team is working hard.
L aura shoots and scores again.
L ucy finishes off the game with a cracking volley.

Katie Moreton (11)
Thomas Telford School, Telford

The British Nation

The British are a complicated nation
and therefore have a strange reputation,
from queuing endlessly without a care
to bowler hats for city gents to wear!

From cucumber sandwiches on a silver platter
to cod and chips in deep-fried batter.
From pieces of toast layered with caviar
to salted peanuts put out on the bar.

From stretch limousines to transport the wealthy
to our double-decker buses that aren't too healthy!
You can risk a train to make you late
or hail a taxi for that special date!

From those that have a 'stiff upper lip'
to those that nod or make their head dip.
From those that smile and say, 'Good day'
to those that like to keep everyone at bay.

As you can see, we're a complicated nation,
there's a definite reason for our reputation
but it wouldn't do for us to be the same,
accepting each other is the name of the game.

Holly Wild (12)
Thomas Telford School, Telford

Heartbroken

Heartbroken is the colour of deep dark green,
Heartbroken is the sight of a distraught scene.
Heartbroken is the result of a constant liar,
Heartbroken is the feeling of an abandoned desire.
Heartbroken is the taste of upset, so wild,
Heartbreak is the loneliness of an orphan child.

Olivia Walmsley (12)
Thomas Telford School, Telford

My Nightmare

The wind howling in my ear
Screaming in my face
Chilling me to the very core
I'm cold, cold, cold . . . *cold*, to the very core.

I feel a twig-like hand,
I turn around and the trees are trying to grab me.
Squeeze me, crush me until my bones have shattered,
Bones broken, smashed or shattered, I will go on.

The darkness fell, like a ton of bricks,
With doors creaking, people screaming.
Windows cackle with laughter
I feel another twig-like hand squeezing my shoulder

The door will wail and howl for evermore
It howled yesterday, it howled last month
It howled as soon as it was built!

The house stares at you
You can't do anything
Nothing at all

I'm scared, I'm cold
I'm cold, cold, cold . . . cold to the very core

I smell food but there is none
I smell hot chocolate . . . but it's all gone.

Melissa Nock (11)
Thomas Telford School, Telford

A Cat's Nightmare

I might be a cat that purrs with affection,
But inside me I pray for protection,
I wish for a family that cares
And loves me,

I want to be free and travel around the world
Meet new people, meet new friends
Maybe start a new beginning

My fur might still be silky and keep me warm,
But I can't survive in a winter's storm,
I hold on to my heart and pray,
That maybe one day I could say,

I might be a cat with no family or friends,
I might have no bed and sleep with the hens,
Yes I might be alone with nothing to eat,
But I know one day I'll meet,

An owner who loves me and hugs me tight,
Who will feed me my favourite dish,
A smelly old fish
And will softly stroke me
And will never leave me.

That will sing me to sleep,
And hold me tight,
And I will remember
All our good times.

Georgia Christodoulou (12)
Thomas Telford School, Telford

Teenage Recipe

Take a body about 14 years old and place in an oven
until skin is greasy and oily.
Leave it to set in a warm dry place.
When set rub in some 'laziness' and 'can't be bothered'.

Next mix in a bowl, a spoonful of 'moodiness',
a pinch of 'anger' and a handful of 'naughtiness'.
Stuff the body till full.

Place about twenty-four spots on a tray,
cover them in 'redness' and 'itchiness' paste.
Cook them until hard and crusty.
When cooked place them on the teenager's face
in the most awkward places.

Grind some 'attitude problem',
grate some 'back-chat' and crush some depression into a powder
and smother it all over the body and leave it to set.

Finally place the body in a nice comfy bed
and don't dare disturb it till at least eleven o'clock the next morning!

Stephanie Rogers (12)
Thomas Telford School, Telford

Autumn

Autumn,
Open-armed with a welcoming face,
Trees dancing to the music of the leaves,
Cool breezes breathing lightly,
Crispy leaves pirouetting across the glistening ground,
Closed windows all steamed up.

Autumn,
Stalking, stalking,
Open-armed, blowing furiously,
Creeping, creeping,
Across the streets, over the rivers,
Autumn has arrived.

Amy Finch (12)
Thomas Telford School, Telford

Can You Help Me?

I sit alone in this dark mine
I feel lonely as I watch the world go by
I question myself, am I alone?
The taste of dust scatters in my mouth
My mouth goes all dry when I'm alone
I am starving
Someone please feed me

As I open my mouth I see a sparkle of blood
As if . . . I was a dead man
I can feel my face as cold as ever
My tear trickles along my face
Like a snake slithering along a cold surface
I can touch dirt on the floor and on the walls
Sometimes I wonder, *if all the dirt fell on me*
Would I be buried alive?
Voices echo in the mine as I wake up
I hear the horse trotting along the metal track
I open the door as it squeaks
I shut the door as I hear a *bang*
I shout, 'Can you help me?'

Luke Hughes (12)
Thomas Telford School, Telford

Time Flies

Why does time never swoop or glide?
When my mind is occupied,
I can safely say time just waltzes by

When I'm soaking wet in my welly boots,
Time goes trudging by.

When I'm lying in my bed
Time is running through my head,
Five minutes is what my mum said
I've got to get to school for eight
Or else I'll be sent to the Head.

Curtis Goodman (12)
Thomas Telford School, Telford

The Man

The man lay in bed looking cold and weak
His eyes turning grey and his lips becoming dry.
The man turned to his daughter with tears
Running down his pale white cheeks. 'I'm scared,' he said,
'I'm scared of dying.'
The man's daughter took him by the hand and said,
'There is no need for you to be scared,
Your family is here for you and will be by your side to the end,
No one will leave you for we love you so much
You have cared for us many times
And now it is time for us to do the same for you.'
The man turned back to his original position,
He then stared at the ceiling
Thinking about what he would leave behind.
There was silence as he drifted out of his old life
Into a better life somewhere else.
His family was sobbing as the nurse took away the cords and wires.
As the man's family left the room his daughter knew
That he would never leave,
He would always be watching over his family
And the man would always be in their hearts
And someday his family would join him in peace and happiness.

Samantha Beresford (12)
Thomas Telford School, Telford

She Wishes For A Teddy Bear

Had I a big fluffy teddy bear
Enwrought with bows and hearts,
The outstanding cuddliness
Of the cutest, biggest, loveable bear.

I would spread its fluffy arms around you,
But I being poor, have not enough money,
I have been in a wonderful daydream,
Without the cutest, loveable bear!

Emma Tranter (12)
Thomas Telford School, Telford

The Inferno

The scarlet blaze roared,
The air crackled,
While the flames danced.
Blood-red, bright orange, exploding yellows,
The colours swirled,
Almost hypnotically blending together.
The sun had come down to Earth,
The blinding light,
The stimulating heat.
The fire blazed overpoweringly,
The burning chill,
Would splinter the shuddering spine.
The massacred chars fluttered,
Silhouetted perfectly.
The inferno was a raging warrior,
Leaping, thrashing, pounding and rushing,
It continues to rampage,
Destroying, polluting and devastating.

Alistair Smith (11)
Thomas Telford School, Telford

My Trusty Mobile

M y lifeline to friends
O ld and new
B eeping, ringing, singing
I put it in my pocket
L eft on vibrate
E xcitement when it rings

P eople I text
H ome calls or not
O n my trusty mobile
N ever without it
E xcept at mealtimes
S o that's my mobile.

Jake Megal (11)
Thomas Telford School, Telford

Tempting Time

Time is like a never-ending line,
Full of both happiness and sadness,
People find it curious time,
Also full of danger.

Time goes on for ages,
Like an endless road of wonder,
Like people flicking through pages,
Who knows what will happen next.

Time is full of happiness,
Time is full of sadness,
Time is full of madness,
Time is happy, sad and mad.

People find time curious,
It occupies their mind,
They want to explore its limits,
To see what they will find.

Many hope to master time,
Their destiny they want to change,
Don't mess with Father Time,
They fail to listen to the warning told.

Kyle Baker (12)
Thomas Telford School, Telford

Sadness

Sadness had gripped my heart,
As happiness had said goodbye.
The feeling made my blood shiver.
The doorstep where I sat wrinkled up,
My body pale as a white sheet of paper.
Fiery skies rape the sleeping beauty
I sit in isolation, bloodthirsty,
My eyes swollen up with bags resting beneath them.
My heart shattered to pieces.
My nails are the hinges of knives,
Scarred the walls who cry in pain and sorrow.
The imagery of clothing, the dead wait silently.
I suddenly rose up,
Next . . .
I rampaged through the street crying,
Then . . .
Bam, bam, neenaw, neenaw . . .
I fall to my knees,
Then to the ground,
I could hardly picture anything, everything was moving.
I clutched onto my heart, it was burning.
My spirit had taken over my life.

Hurneet Kaur Kalirai (11)
Thomas Telford School, Telford

Bullying

I am being bullied every day
I feel like the colour grey
I wish sometimes I wasn't here
Every day I shake with fear
I go home to bed and lay awake
I think of what they'll do the next day
They talk about me the next day
I can hear everything that they say
I start to cry
And wish that I could die
I hear them shout
They bully me day in, day out
I've had enough
I have got to stay tough
The head teacher sees me
And offers to buy me a cup of tea
He sits me down and we have a talk
Then we go out for a walk
He sorts it out
They don't bully me day in or day out
I have made new friends
The bullying ends
I am very pleased
I am no longer teased.

Jade Brownhill (11)
Thomas Telford School, Telford

Dreams Of Christmas

Dream of . . .
Holly upon the Christmas tree,
Mistletoe hanging high,
Dancing at the Christmas dance,
We love it so much but why?

Maybe because . . .
The fresh smell of Christmas,
The presents make you feel great,
The thought of cooked turkey and Christmas dinner,
And giving gifts to your best mate.

Maybe because . . .
Of Christmas dances,
Having seasonal fun with friends,
Having snow fights with next-door neighbours,
The seasonal fun never ends.

Dream of . . .
Holly upon the Christmas tree,
Mistletoe hanging high,
Dancing at the Christmas dance,
We love it so much that's why!

Andrea Field (12)
Thomas Telford School, Telford

My Butterfly

My butterfly flutters by performing a merry dance,
Collecting nectar from lots of flowers and plants.
Flying around doing its daily good deeds,
Carrying pollen to produce heaps of nuts and seeds.
Many bright colours flying in the sky,
What a beautiful sight in my eye.
It disappears when it's time to say goodnight,
Returning tomorrow when the sun shines bright.

Kellie Appleby (13)
Thomas Telford School, Telford

The Chase

Watching with its eyes,
And scratching with its claws,
Leaping after the rodent
With its soft and padded paws.

Scratches down a tree trunk,
An empty bowl of food,
A mouse that's run away now,
It's in a wicked mood.

The mice squeak from the garden,
They've managed to escape,
And now they'll all go run and hide,
Before it's again too late.

It knows it's time for sleep,
The creature comes back in,
Yet although the mice go out to play,
The chase will soon begin.

Lily Penfold (12)
Thomas Telford School, Telford

Make Poverty History

Every year since the world began,
Families have been torn to shreds,
Not just because of the natural world,
But the lack of food and medication needed,
Still to this very day there is not enough support given
To those who are struggling to survive,
The food that is wasted in the UK,
Is enough to keep many alive,
Most of the victims are children,
These children don't even get to live to the age of five years old,
But that can all stop, if you have a heart of gold!

Abbie Bailey (11)
Thomas Telford School, Telford

Ball Of Light

The world is a ball, colourful and bright,
Killing the Earth as it moans and cries,
Halo of light suffering as it wears away,
Sticks trembling on the Earth as it whimpers,
Dark and silent, wrinkles upon its face,
Blue ink splattered on the surface,
Ball of fire crowding the darkness,
As the Earth is tearing, tearing away,
Embarrassed is the Earth everything it fears,
As the ball of light whispers it hears,
World is sad, sad is he,
Aerosol cans destroying the halo,
Pollutants warming the Earth's atmosphere,
Weeping noisily, destroyers slaughter the exterior,
Sticks upon the halo destructive some can be,
As the shadow creeps over the icy blanket of the world,
Cubes of bricks pressed on the ground,
The world around us is dying, shame upon the world.

Danielle Bowater (11)
Thomas Telford School, Telford

Bullying

Bullying is when . . .
You are left out,
You are called names.
You must tell someone, no doubt.

Bullying is when . . .
You are hurt,
You are forced to give your pocket money.
That's the money you have earned.

A bully is . . .
Someone who is cruel to weaker people.
Someone that has nothing else better to do.
Someone that needs to be set straight.

Kalpna Ahir (13)
Thomas Telford School, Telford

Mysteries Of Life

The yellow sun gets poisoned
And turns a misty grey,
I think it looks like a distorted ghost
But many a folk say, 'Nay!'

I stare up to his twinkling companions
And see how they shine so bright,
However when some days they aren't there
It gives me an awful fright!

I sometimes think and wonder
Of how mysterious it can be,
Of how a black sheet covers the land
As if there's a special key!

A key that lets the world into darkness
And another one by day,
Oh how I love my life,
Oh how I treasure each day.

Vicki Wood (12)
Thomas Telford School, Telford

The Thunderstorm

Spears sent from Zeus,
God's anger and rage,
An explosion in the sky,
A devil stepping foot on Heaven,
Terror and danger,
Bombs falling on Earth's core,
The sound of a lion's roar,
A powerplant gone wrong,
Black smoke trailing all around,
The smell of ashes and burnt rocks,
Rays of plasma light scraping the ground!
The final acts of . . .
The thunderstorm.

Tyler Thomas (11)
Thomas Telford School, Telford

My Funny Poem

Oh how I yearn to walk again
under the glistening sun
but since my leg is in a cast
I cannot walk or run!

Spring has sprung, the air is open
flowers in full bloom
yet still, alas I sit here and mope
stuck up in my room.

So I turn to writing poems
I try to make them funny
like what on earth would you do
if the sun was not so sunny?

Hobbling all around the house
and crawling on my knees
I cannot reach my beloved chocolate
could someone help me please?

I stare most of the time
looking at my chocolate
this horror is unbearable
can my luck be this bad?

I sit and watch reality TV
to waste my days away
I'm sure it comes as no surprise
it is the highlight of my day

I could tell you about Superman
my girlfriend's stash of comics
but alas I haven't got the time
because I'm hooked on Stereophonics.

So, be oh so gentle with your words
for it's not the final hour
I hope this entry is early enough
so that you won't be oh so sour!

Liam Sullivan (12)
Thomas Telford School, Telford

Mysterious Atmosphere

The trees gather around
Sheltering me from the splintering rain,
I cower as they scrape my skin with their branches
And shudder as their leaves flutter and scatter to the ground.

The sun glimmers through the branches
Causing me to squint precariously,
The gentle heat and rain creates a tingling sensation all over my skin
Strange sounds echoing through the still air.

Birds twitter in the trees
Searching desperately for food,
Soaring high above all people and trees
Fading inconspicuously into the sunlight.

The damp, mossy grass
Smothers the hard floor, dangerously,
The sinister shadows surround me
I hear the wind screech.

The babbling brook flows constantly
Trickling, bubbling and frothing,
Down the rough, jagged and irregular stones
The sound relaxes me, allowing me to daydream.

The forest is empty, a lonely place
Desolate and deserted, a dreary surrounding,
Monotonous trees and intriguing sounds.

A mysterious atmosphere
Which many do not enter?

Rachael Holyhead (12)
Thomas Telford School, Telford

Friends

You're
My friend
My companion
Through good times and bad
My friend, my buddy
Through happy times and sad,
Beside me you stand
Beside me you walk
You're there for me to listen,
You're there for me to talk
With happiness, with smiles
With pain and tears,
I know you'll be there
Throughout many years!

Daniel Goodall (13)
Thomas Telford School, Telford

Sun's Rays

The sun's rays
Light up the whole world
A warm blanket over us,
The heat of the fire
Covers the Sahara Desert,
With the soft whisky sand
And a beach ball too
With the end of the day
The *sunset!*

Samantha Lunn (11)
Thomas Telford School, Telford

Rainbows

R ain starts and the sun comes out
something strange appears
A ll different colours, 7 I think,
all in a curved-shaped bridge.
I t's called a rainbow and appears when
sun and rain both meet.
N ow a rainbow has appeared
for me and you to see.
B lue and green, pink and yellow,
many bright colours contained.
O nly can be seen in the day,
up high in the sky.
W hen the sun goes in, the rainbow fades,
and the sky's left grey or blue.
S o now you know how a rainbow occurs.

Shazia Bano-Shah (12)
Thomas Telford School, Telford

Stars

Star light, star bright,
Shining in the wondrous night,
In the black velvet sky,
With comets and meteors passing by,
I look at the endless stars
Just like I look at rushing cars,
Bright and glittering with the moon,
What will happen to it all soon?
I sit and stare
Without a care,
As I bury my face in my hands.

Kate Breeze (12)
Thomas Telford School, Telford

Time

Time is like the rising sun,
It has many chances, you only have one,
But one day it will die too.

When you are in your prime,
Take your chances as they come as you may live to regret,
So remember you are not like the rising sun.

Every day you are getting older,
The time ticking by,
So remember you are not like the rising sun.

Time is like the rising sun,
It has many chances, you only have one,
But one day it will die too.

Reece Smith (12)
Thomas Telford School, Telford

Reading Out Loud!

I stand at the front,
Looking out at the back wall.
Yet my eyes seem to be drawn,
To look at them all.

I try to speak,
Yet my voice is on hold.
My hands go all sweaty,
I'm far from being bold.

My heart's beating fast,
And they're all still waiting,
For a poem that may end,
With a young girl fainting.

Emmie Edwards (11)
Thomas Telford School, Telford

The House That Lived . . .

Darkness filled the sky, as,
Rain pelted down like a hammer to a nail,
Thunder crashed and lightning struck,
As trees danced in the gale.

I walked up the crumbling path,
The tree's bony fingers, reached out and stroked me,
Its tall body stood strong against the wind,
Guarding the house.

It seemed to be late for its own funeral.
Its splintered door creaked as it welcomed me in.
Its windows showed the face of a terrified thirteen-year-old,
Its mirror tells a thousand tales from times of scary old.

Its floorboards creaked,
Its guests squeaked, as if warning me to *beware!*
I ran, ran, ran, till all of a sudden . . .

Darkness filled the sky,
Rain pelted down like a hammer to a nail,
Thunder crashed and lightning struck,
As trees danced in the gale.

Gemma Maybury (11)
Thomas Telford School, Telford

Life Behind Bars

Here I am behind my bars
I might as well be on planet Mars
How I wish I could be free
Like the people I can see

The same routine day in day out
Long and boring without a doubt
A whistle goes, I have to react
The same old tricks like an acrobat

Food and water in plentiful supply
But freedom calls, I wish I could fly
The lights go out, it's time to sleep
I sit here quietly without a cheep

Another day dawns and the door is open
It's my chance to escape like I've been hoping
Alas it's just the same routine
I've been let out my cage so it can be cleaned

My feathers are ruffled; I'm back in my cage
I've been flapping around in a nervous rage
But because I know life as a budgie is sweet
I'll just sit here and go *tweet, tweet, tweet.*

Stuart Dunlop (11)
Thomas Telford School, Telford

The Two Paths

As I was travelling through the forest,
The two paths diverged,
One dark, one unworn, alive as a party without the people,
But with the animals instead.

I stop and think, which one to take.
Looking down a path,
I can see it as far as it bends then it disappears into the distance.
The leaves and the undergrowth, the mud under your feet.

I choose the bright path.
It was only fair, to see all of its pure beauty,
As I walk down its path,
I seem to join its party.

As it comes to an end,
With a wall of trees.
I sigh and wonder,
Wonder where I would be if . . .
If I had taken that other path,
I cannot come back,
Only look forward to what will be.

Laura Roberts (11)
Thomas Telford School, Telford

She Wishes For A Big Fluffy Teddy Bear

Had I a big fluffy teddy bear,
Enwrought with stitches and fluff,
The golden brown fur and the red ribbon round its neck.
Of the glowing black eyes and the little pink mouth.

I would cuddle the big fluffy teddy bear;
But I, being selfish, have only one for myself;
I have imagined this teddy bear for years;
But now, my wishes may never come true.

Carly-Jade Newnes (12)
Thomas Telford School, Telford

Insanity

My heart thuds,
My brain stops,
My eyes blur,
What did you say to me?
Are you stalking my wife?
Argh!
The trees are whispering to each other,
Talking mutinous declarations.

The nurses are there,
They're not helping,
They're making it worse.

The children are coming, Alex!
They're singing and riding animals,
They're coming for you.

They say I'm insane,
Locked up in this cell,
They think I'm insane for the things I can see,
But they're the ones that are insane for not seeing them.

Alex Davies (13)
Trinity Catholic School, Leamington Spa

Guilt

Guilt makes you feel locked up,
As if you are never going to get out.
Guilt is being stuck in Hell,
As if you are never going to get out.
Guilt does not let you look up,
You always have to look down.
Guilt is a burden,
That you are never going to get out.
Guilt!

Katie O'Kelly (13)
Trinity Catholic School, Leamington Spa

Determination

The dawn of a challenge emerging from night
The last stars fading from sapphire skies
A horizon tinged red with filtering light
The journey begins with a gold sunrise.

Prepare to set out on a fearsome path
Enter a world where dangers thrive
Break through the clutch of darkness' wrath
Fight for goodness - and survive.

Venture through the forests and tundra
Race through wind and surge across tides
Be a master of fire and thunder
See how the power of wilderness glides.

Remember the goal you're striving to meet
Know where your courage and loyalties lie
Be ready to combat a terrifying feat
Let your heart guide you - you have to try.

The road is long, flooded with fear
The blackness of doubt streams icily past
All light, all hope may disappear
If you give up, you will not last.

Blazing sparks flare in your eyes
Your blood runs warm with fiery cause
Determination drowns out evil cries
Like a tiger's, your spirit roars.

Hannah Quayle (13)
Trinity Catholic School, Leamington Spa

Sad

Sadness is when my friends do not talk to me.
Sadness is when I argue with Mum.
Sadness is when I lose something special.
Sadness is when I am all alone.
Sadness is when I finish a poem.

Nandylola Lloyd (13)
Trinity Catholic School, Leamington Spa

The Wonderful Life Of Me!

One is throwing your dinner on the floor when you're in
                                                    your high chair,
Two is taking your first steps and falling flat on your face,
Three is having a stress at Daddy when he won't fix your
Farmyard and then banging your head on the fireplace,
Four is learning to ride your bike with stabilisers but still falling off,
Five is going to school to meet your friends and make
Christmas cards and getting glitter all over your hands and face,
Six is being an angel in the Christmas play and falling over
And pushing everyone else over with you,
Seven is playing 'Rugrats' with your friends and always being Lil,
Eight is getting a brand new bike then scratching the paintwork,
Nine is going to Australia and bouncing on the trampoline,
Then falling on my dad's cousin's dog,
Ten is drinking Bucks Fizz for the first time on my birthday,
Eleven is going to secondary school and feeling scared
Because there are so many big people,
Twelve is having more and more stresses at your parents.

Jessica Clack (13)
Trinity Catholic School, Leamington Spa

Home Is . . .

The smell of home cooking.
Stroking the purring tabby cat by the fire.
Watching Corrie.
Snuggling up in bed in the winter.
Waking up on Crimbo morning
And going out to play in the refreshingly cold snow.
Where you took your first steps.
Where your dad wrecked the barbecue in the scorching summer.
Where you and your mum made fairy cakes when you were small.
Where your first birthday was.
Where you feel safe.
A place full of happy memories.

Lilly Aaron (12)
Trinity Catholic School, Leamington Spa

Through The Years

One is when you eat your mum's face cream,
Two is when you stop using your potty,
Three is when you dislocate your thumb and you faint,
Four is when you start school and make some friends
                    called Sophie and Melissa,
Five is when you learn to ride a bike,
Six is when you go to a birthday party and you eat
                    all the sugary sweets off the cake,
Seven is when you find out Father Christmas isn't real,
Eight is when you fall out with your best friends,
                    Melissa and Charlotte,
Nine is when you have your first boyfriend called Ben,
Ten is when you go on an adventure holiday with your school,
Eleven is when you move to a bigger house,
Twelve is when your dog has to be put down.

Dulcie McFadden (13)
Trinity Catholic School, Leamington Spa

A Special Valley In The Countryside

There lies a place far away, overflowing with fresh green grass
Where the gentle air swishes through my hair
And the flute-like melody of swirling swallows rings out
As they ebb and flow through the soft blue sky
I dip my hand into the smooth emerald grass
And I open my ears to hear the water splashing upstream in the river
The towering trees sway side to side in the fresh morning breeze
This makes me feel calm
The sapphire blue river crashes down,
Exploding upon massive rocks beneath and I am fascinated
The spiralling swallows swoop down,
Dashing and darting over the river, catching flies
And the fresh air is absolutely extraordinary for me.
I feel at peace with my grandma next to me
I feel happy.

David Myers Nava (13)
Trinity Catholic School, Leamington Spa

Happiness

Happiness is the frosty white snow falling on your window ledge,
Settling like icing sugar on a mince pie.

Happiness is the clear blue sea lapping at the sandy shore.

Happiness is the silver disc moon hanging in the velvet sky.

Happiness is the red and orange sunset,
Setting the clouds on fire.

Happiness is the first spring plant,
Shooting out of the ground.

Sarah-Jane Wilson (13)
Trinity Catholic School, Leamington Spa

13-Year-Old Girl

13 is trying to earn enough money to buy a new mobile,
13 is always stopping out with your mates and not
                                    wanting to go home,
13 is studying to try and get top marks in your SATs,
13 is shopping for a new outfit for the valentine disco,
13 is turning into a teenager and taking on more responsibilities,
13 is realising that you can't get away with the things you used to,
13 is having a girlie night in with your sister Maisie.

Zoe Ransley (13)
Trinity Catholic School, Leamington Spa

Anger Is . . .

Someone getting mad and frustrated,
Being out of control,
Screaming and shouting at someone,
Slamming the door violently behind you,
Taking advantage of you.

Lee Sharpe (13)
Trinity Catholic School, Leamington Spa

Childhood

1 is when you jump on the cat, making it angry and getting bitten,
2 is when you discover putting your toast in the video player
                                                    isn't a good idea,
3 is discovering the beautiful taste of mud cakes,
4 is climbing up the oak tree and realising you can't get back down,
5 is causing mayhem in the classroom and starting a paint fight,
6 is exploring the wonders of the world. Why?
7 is playing kiss chase in the playground and making
                                        all the boys run away,
8 is wanting to be the best in the talent show, falling off the stage
                                        and making a fool of yourself,
9 is your birthday party, eating all the sweets and
                                        regretting it the next day,
10 is going on holiday, plunging into the sea, and getting stung
                                                    by a jellyfish,
11 is experiencing secondary school, everything's so big
                                        and you're so little,
12 is kissing childhood goodbye, starting to put your lipgloss on,
                and throwing those tantrums your mum and dad
                                are going to have to get used to,
You're changing!

Sinead Healy (13)
Trinity Catholic School, Leamington Spa

Anger

Anger is like a kettle - once you switch it on,
It gets hotter and hotter until it blows a fuse.

Anger is like your blood boiling through your body.

Anger is when a baby loses its brand new toy.

Anger is hiding your own feelings.

Anger, it's like when your new girlfriend dumps you for an older man.

Jacob Reed (13)
Trinity Catholic School, Leamington Spa

When I Was . . .

13 is getting your first job and being so excited about your
                                        pay cheque
13 is chasing a boy you have no chance with,
13 is studying so hard for your SATs you fall asleep on
                                        your science book
13 is getting your birthday money and spending it all on clothes,
13 is sleeping over at Sophie's house and chilling out,
13 is watching sex scenes with your parents and
                                        getting so embarrassed,
13 is when you get fired for the first time and you feel so down,
13 is when you get acne and everyone stares at you,
13 is having a sleepover and dancing round in your Pjs,
13 is getting a Terrier and chasing after it when it runs away,
13 is getting your haircut at Toni & Guy's and breaking
                                        your mum's bank.
13 is a fabulous/great/emotional/devastating age.

Aimee Scanlon (14)
Trinity Catholic School, Leamington Spa

Twelve-Year-Old Girl Is . . .

Liking boys more and more for the first time,
Staying out late with mates,
Falling out now and then with girls over silly things,
Being able to have your own mobile,
Almost becoming a teenager,
Parents trusting you to go into town,
Having your first boyfriend,
More pocket money like £15 or £20,
Doing chores just to get a little bit more pocket money,
Having sleepovers on the weekend with mates,
Staying up really late to watch horror movies,
Being lazy and waking up at eleven or twelve o'clock in the morning!

Kayleigh Randall (12)
Trinity Catholic School, Leamington Spa

Imagination

Imagination is a chance to be creative,
It is to imagine inventively.

Imagination is a new character,
It is not copying something.

Imagination is special,
It is like having an unseen higher power.

Imagination is a rainbow,
It is many colours to form dreams.

Imagination is a walk through the park,
It is letting your mind run wild.

Emily Murphy (13)
Trinity Catholic School, Leamington Spa

Anger

A nger is fury bursting into flames,
N ever knowing when to lash out or keep it in,
G oing red when it's building up inside you,
E very drop of blood turning to boiling point,
R eally starting to build up inside you and then finally
        anger is *no* more!

Arthur Bradley (13)
Trinity Catholic School, Leamington Spa

Guilt

Guilt is worrying about what you've done,
Guilt is the cloud that blocks out the sun,
It stops you sleeping, it makes you regret,
It happens when you lie, cheat and want to forget.

Guilt is having a conscience.

Katherine Horrocks (13)
Trinity Catholic School, Leamington Spa

A 12-Year-Old Boy Is . . .

Playing rugby
Going to high school
Looking at girls
Messing around
Being independent,
Going down town,
Hanging around with older mates,
Watching football,
Beginning to have spots,
Being cheeky,
Trying smoking,
Playing PS2 games.

Alex Norman (12)
Trinity Catholic School, Leamington Spa

Happy

H aving everything you've always wished for,
A lways having a laugh,
P laying with your mates,
P erfect in all ways,
Y ou're always in a great mood.

Kayleigh Walsh (13)
Trinity Catholic School, Leamington Spa

Anger

Anger is red-hot fire which burns your emotions,
Anger is the feeling when you just want to kill,
Anger is a bull charging at a red cape,
Anger is clammy fists ready to lash out,
Anger comes from within.

Harley Stanley (13)
Trinity Catholic School, Leamington Spa

Twelve-Year-Old Boy Is . . .

Playing rugby,
Trying smoking,
Getting spots,
Going down town,
Making mates older than you,
Arm-wrestling,
Messing around,
Liking girls,
Playing PS2,
Being independent,
Being cheeky,
Going to secondary school.

Lewis Bromwich (12)
Trinity Catholic School, Leamington Spa

Twelve-Year-Old Girl Is . . .

Noticing which boys are cute,
Watching horror movies with your mates,
Playing out late and hanging around,
Allowed to go to town and camping with friends at weekends,
Hating school apart from catching up with gossip at social times,
Having loads of sleepovers and inviting boys round to your home,
Having your own mobile for home and outings,
Slapping on loads of make-up to go out to clubs,
Getting £25 pounds each month and getting hyper on pop
                                        and sweets,
Parents trust you more and believe you are being good!
Going to bed late on weekends and school nights too,
Your parents letting you go on MSN Hotmail until midnight.

Lianne Davis (12)
Trinity Catholic School, Leamington Spa

Twelve-Year-Old Boy Is . . .

Riding my jet-black bike fast at Newbold Comlyn with
My mates Peter, John and Elliot,
Playing rugby at Harbury with my mates Joe and Sam,
Playing football with my mates Tom and Ryan,
Going to bed at ten and not wanting to get up in the morning,
Enjoying spaghetti Bolognese, pizza, McDonald's and ice cream,
Hating my school uniform which is black, yellow, purple and white,
Watching 'Pimp My Ride' and 'The Bill'.
Getting the best phone - the Samsung D500,
Having two brothers, Thomas and Kieran and sister called Lily-Jo,
Drinking Coca-Cola,
Having a best friend called Marco,
Playing rugby at school and getting all muddy.

Daniel Brennan (12)
Trinity Catholic School, Leamington Spa

Twelve-Year-Old Boy Is . . .

Starting secondary school and being scared!
Checking out the girls and finding out who's cute,
Watching TV all the time,
My favourite programme is 'Pimp My Ride',
Playing football and learning new tricks,
Going up town with your mates,
Getting the newest phone out for your birthday - Samsung D500,
Starting to grow taller than your parents,
Getting £10 pocket money for being good,
Playing on Fifa 06, the newest game on your PlayStation 2
And not coming off it,
Sitting on the cream sofa and being really lazy,
Going to bed at 11 o'clock and not wanting to get up in the morning,
Having fights with my little brother Harry.

Ryan Billington (12)
Trinity Catholic School, Leamington Spa

13-Year-Old Boy

13 is when you wear cool clothes and think you're cool,
13 is when you wear very expensive jewellery and
                               think you're hard,
13 is when you get better at football and think you're
                               Zinedine Zidane,
13 is when you start ignoring your parents and thinking
                               you can get away with it,
13 is when you start wasting credit on your mobile,
                               ringing your friends,
13 is when you try having a cigarette and end up choking on it,
13 is when you try flirting with girls but end up getting slapped,
13 is when you have to start cleaning your room by yourself,
13 is when you have to start concentrating hard in classes
                               because you have important tests,
13 is when you start picking on younger kids and
                               think you're strong,
13 is when you start coming home late at night,
13 is when you use slang instead of proper language,
13 is when you become older and everything in your life changes.

Lucio-Tommaso Abinanti (13)
Trinity Catholic School, Leamington Spa

Happiness

H aving everything you've always wished for,
A gigantic house with a swimming pool,
P laying with friends - James, Arthur and Alex,
P leasing your family and making them proud,
I pods growing on trees!
N ever being sad or scared about life,
E ating all the sweets you want without gaining weight,
S leeping in a warm, cosy bed,
S upporting Celtic as they are an amazing team!

George Coady (13)
Trinity Catholic School, Leamington Spa

A Twelve-Year-Old Boy

Going into town,
Getting spots,
Playing for a proper football team,
Liking rap music,
Playing the PS2 a lot,
Understanding films,
Becoming cheeky,
Asking great questions,
Seeing girls in a different light,
Thinking of great questions,
Making my own breakfast,
Buying my own stuff.

James Lawless (12)
Trinity Catholic School, Leamington Spa

Anger

Anger is when you're burnt up with hate,
Never knowing when you will lash out,
Getting angry feels good,
Every time after you feel bad,
Remembering what you did.

Keir Sayce (13)
Trinity Catholic School, Leamington Spa

Hatred

Hatred is an emotion,
Hatred is death,
Hatred is starting wars,
Hatred is tearing families apart,
Hatred is powerful.

Archie Skelcher (13)
Trinity Catholic School, Leamington Spa

Twelve-Year-Old Boy

A part is being cool,
Going to town with your mates,
Playing footie with your mates,
Not listening to your parents,
Going to parties with your mates,
Thankfully saying 'I've done my chores.'
Not wanting to do my homework,
Buying a mobile and getting loads of cred,
Not listening to teachers,
Buying clothing instead of toys,
Staying up late on your own.

Mitchell Morris (12)
Trinity Catholic School, Leamington Spa

Twelve-Year-Old Girl Is . . .

When I start secondary school and I am dead scared,
When I am now one of the big ones even though I am tiny,
When I play netball with our teacher at the school,
When I am fantastic at dance,
When I get loads of pocket money like £10 or £15 pounds,
When I get a new phone called 'Mini Lobster'.
When I get lots of homework like English, maths, science,
When the teacher shouts at me, 'Get out of the classroom now!'
When I go out after school into town with my friends,
When some girls are great at football,
When I am spoilt as I am the only girl with four brothers,
When I can enjoy being 12 for a whole 12 months.

Shannon Marie Byrne (12)
Trinity Catholic School, Leamington Spa

Twelve-Year-Old Girl . . .

Is
When you start liking boys for the first time and thinking who's cute.
Is
When your parents trust you going into the local town with your mates.
Is
When you get £20 pocket money for doing chores such as washing up, setting the table and going around the shop.
Is
When you receive the latest Motorola mobile and pay-as-you-go yourself.
Is
When you begin an activity and you get really good at it.
Is
When you figure you need make-up, mascara, blusher and the rest.
Is
When you start taking forever doing your hair.
Is
When your parents ask you to come back at nine and you come back at ten.
Is
When you become really, really cheeky to your teachers.
Is
When your mum tells you to clean your room because it's a mess.
Is
When you get your first after school detention.
Is
When you ask for money off your parents and they say, 'No!'

Lauren Ransford (12)
Trinity Catholic School, Leamington Spa

Animals!

Animals have feelings too,
Just like me and just like you.
Vivisection is wrong,
So just stand up and be strong,
Stand up for your pets
And support the vets.

Hunting is nasty and terrible,
So help ban it and be sensible,
Zoos are mean and wrong,
They have been around for too long,
Circuses are cruel,
So be cool and
Stop them straight away.

Nicole Corrigan (12)
Woodfield Middle School, Redditch

Einstein Year

Einstein! What a mastermind.
Didn't you know? You must be blind.
He was born in March 1879,
He was a genius before his first whine,
When he was born the doctor said,
'This baby has a weird-shaped head!'
He discovered that $E=MC^2$,
Went out into the street and everybody stared,
One hundred years have gone now,
He died in 1955,
Let's remember this special day,
When he changed the whole world's way.

Mariya Arshad (12)
Woodfield Middle School, Redditch

Alien, Alien

In space, on a planet, sits an alien, alien, alien,
With its tentacles and sharp teeth, alien, alien,
Its disguise is so clever, alien or not, alien, alien,
Eats people, abducts people, watch out people! Alien, alien,
Leave us alone, or oh no, you will be gone forever! Alien, alien,
Don't come closer, stay away, *argh!*
I've had a lovely meal thank you,
Me, alien, alien, I've eaten you!

Daniella Gregg (11)
Woodfield Middle School, Redditch

Einstein

E instein is a mastermind,
I deally never leaves his brain behind
N ever forgets that E=MC²
S ometimes people think
T hat they should be scared!
E instein is one great man,
I nterestingly enough, he's brainier than my nan!
N o one I know is the exact same man.

Jayna Chauhan (12)
Woodfield Middle School, Redditch

Planet

P lanning on where to land,
L anding softly,
A tmosphere eye-catching,
N ext discovery found,
E xperimenting to see if it is a life form,
T rying to find life here in space.

Bradley Jones (11)
Woodfield Middle School, Redditch

Parents! Children!

Another day dawns and the story begins
Get up now and get ready for school
Parents nag children for their sins
Come on, you're going to be late for school.

Get up now and get ready for school
(I really wish you'd shut up and go away!)
Come on, you're going to be late for school
I'm up - (not really - I can't face this day.)

I really wish you'd shut up and go away!
Stop being stupid - come down here
I'm up - (not really - I can't face this day)
Come on - there's nothing to fear.

Stop being stupid - come down here
You are always nagging me
Come on - there's nothing to fear
All I want is to be free.

You are always nagging me
Oh! Just change the record will you?
All I want is to be free
Well I'd really like that too!

Oh! Just change the record will you?
Always moaning about my mess
All I want is to be free
Fine then, stay in bed - don't dress.

Always moaning about my mess
Another day dawns and the story begins
Fine then, stay in bed - don't dress
Children nag parents for their sins!

Leigh Todd & Jodie Bough (12)
Woodfield Middle School, Redditch

Parents - Why?

Why are they so annoying?
All they do is nag
Parents - why do we need them?
When they're done, I'm wrung out like a rag!

All they do is nag
Am I really so bad?
When they're done, I'm wrung out like a rag!
They just make me so mad.

Am I really so bad?
It's just a phase I'm going through
They just make me so mad,
I just need someone to talk to.

It's just a phase I'm going through
I'm sure I'll grow out of it
I just need someone to talk to
To lift me out of this pit.

I'm sure I'll grow out of it
Maybe someone will help me
To lift me out of this pit
I wonder who that will be.

Maybe someone will help me
I don't really want to be like this
I wonder who that will be
To turn it around with a kiss.

I don't really want to be like this
Why are they so annoying?
To turn it around with a kiss
Parents - why do we need them?

Cassie Larkin (12) & James King (13)
Woodfield Middle School, Redditch

Space, The Wonderful Things

Fly up, up, up and away,
You could see the Milky Way.

Up in space you will have the chance,
Have the chance to sing and dance.

Discover things that no one has found,
Discover these things on the ground.

When you come back you want to go up again,
But your chances of going up have gone down the drain.

Space, space the wonderful things,
You can go up there in your dreams.

Ben Hyde (11)
Woodfield Middle School, Redditch

My Great Planet

G oodies flying everywhere,
R ain that might just burn your hair,
E verything is good and sweet,
A ll but the weather, dark and meek,
T hen all of a sudden the Skittle rainbow appeared.

P eople on Earth are fussy and loud,
L ost on the planet there isn't a sound,
A ll the time there can't be trouble,
N ot even underneath all that rubble,
E asy as pie, piece of cake,
T here is a chance in this dream, you will not wake . . .

Dale Seel (11)
Woodfield Middle School, Redditch

Animal Cruelty Poem

All these creatures doomed to die,
A chicken in its pen, a pig in its sty.

Waiting for that dreadful day,
When the van comes and takes them away.

Living in fear,
No one loving near,
Can't shed a tear,
Everyone's too near.

Eyes sore, legs broke,
Can't howl or we will choke.

Lying there all alone,
Never shown always thrown.

Please help these animals with no voice,
They can't scream out, they have no choice!

Danielle Fenton (12)
Woodfield Middle School, Redditch

Frozen Love

A drop
Drips off the icicle
A tear
Trickles down my face
Because of
You.

Grace Farrington (15)
Woodlands Community School, Derby

Naked Thoughts

How long will it take for your soul to stop searching,
To give up on faith,
And all that fills its desire?
Just thinking and wondering,
Thoughts rapidly tumbling out.
Tumbling into a deep, black pit beneath it
Filled with hatred, love and sorrow.
To lose confidence and feel nothing forever
Become bare and naked
Your naked thoughts.

How long will it take for your thoughts to surrender?
Never to look back on what hasn't been done
Never to think of what never will happen
And never to be sure.
Surrendering to everything
Living for nothing
Becoming what is not
What never will be
Become bare and naked
Your naked thoughts.

How long until you truly believe
When your soul and your thoughts combine
A never-ending chain of love and hate?
Pure love, sacrificing for tomorrow
Hate, never to know what life intends.
A life where nothing continues, to know it will never end
To know it will die.
Just how long until your thoughts emerge
To combine into all?
From naked to living.
Your thoughts of life.

Katy Harlow (14)
Woodlands Community School, Derby

Yellow Echoes

Rolling over, away from you.
Prop myself, mumble in a thick breath,
'It's almost morning.' You grunt, eyes slits.
Stumble over victims of (the) last night.
I treasure this nothing that happened.

And then the sympathetic dawn light,
Guiding this field of memories.
Though, in my memories, it's a week of nights.
My pace quickens to a swagger,
I'm prancing over the spreading, dead, tripping arms.

Goodbye is smudged by my wails, your tails,
Of course, your smile slides first.
'It's never over,' seems realer than each other.
Watching you go seems ridiculous. Unimaginable.
Now it's all I know of you.

'Home is where the heart is,' a smirking jibe at my grief
I'm not laughing.
But midnight messages and firelight pull back my grins.
He was here before you, what do you know of me but bliss?
And I'm struggling to find even that to offer you.

Warm eyes, positioned so only I notice them.
Breath in my frozen ear, and I'm forever laughing.
Repression isn't so bad, I'm learning to savour it.
And then. Your distant voice, boring into the same ear,
Can you tell? Maybe, I pray, it's the same for you.

Yellow ink like guilt dripping, staining (but you'd strain to notice it)

And we're closer than anyone you know.
Like hysteria, I'm laughing again.

Kate Turner (16)
Woodlands Community School, Derby

In The Pram

Tears well atop rosy, round cheeks,
A bear lies motionless and lost,
Amongst a forest of pacing, polished shoes,
Sticky hands grope a gap and fall short,
Of rescue.

He looks to the heavens,
His creator, a stream of news,
Eagerly spilling her pride,
Upon an old friend, he's unfamiliar,
They discuss those they are meant to love.

'I need you,' he shouts to himself,
Wordless speech escaping his lips,
Hindered by youth and innocence,
A language she will never know,
She does not care.

The boy writhes in his chains,
His face contorted in agony,
A siren piercing and reaching,
Yet unanswered. She knows this call,
And rolls her eyes in shame.

Then the wheels begin to turn,
Driving a shuddering fear,
And as they turn the corner,
A bond is broken, a void forged,
Between carer and toy.

Julian Esposito (15)
Woodlands Community School, Derby

Six Feet Under

As I watch the dull dense object
Slowly float into the cold, lifeless abyss
All I can think of is nothing
For the life I lead will never compare
I'm only one speck of the human race
Yet here I am standing, waiting.

The dark six feet that surround you
Closing in faster choking your every breath
Yet what breath? That last drop seeping out,
Paler now, no colour on that flesh
Yet here we are standing, waiting.

That dull dense object covered in depth
Life that surrounds the mist fading
For what was has now been and gone
Age is of no concern to that cold bleak face
No miseries will ever touch those pale lips
Yet tears are shed while standing here, waiting.

Flowers paraded through hollow paths
Hollow meanings that float through dense air,
Emotions buried immersed, a dark fearful shadow
People's conversations are pointless, immoral
No daring souls, say what you feel
Yet no, we just stand here, waiting.

For the six feet that cover you now,
Will never compare to thousands of hours that I will miss you.

Emily Boyer (15)
Woodlands Community School, Derby